GOD'S
presence
ILLUMINATED

Treasured Thoughts to Inspire
Hope and Light

Christine M. Fisher

90 devotions to help you see God
in the ordinary things of life

God's Presence Illuminated
Treasured Thoughts to Inspire Hope and Light
Christine M. Fisher

To contact the author:
christine@hopetoinspireyou.com
www.hopetoinspireyou.com

Published by:

Mary Ethel

Mary Ethel Eckard
Frisco, Texas

ISBN (Print): 978-1-7338233-7-1
ISBN (E-book): 978-1-7338233-8-8

CONTENTS

DEDICATION

God began placing special people in my path who shared Him through the written word for which I am grateful. With their encouragement and assistance, I embarked on this writing experience penning weekly thoughts on my website, www.hopetoinspireyou.com.

This compilation is dedicated, with gratitude, to all
those who have supported my messages
and encouraged me to put my thoughts into
book form. Thank you and God bless.

FOREWORD

The day started like every other Thursday. As I drove to church for our weekly "group" meeting, I wondered what topics we would discuss. We only have one rule: we can talk about anything as long as we remain friends.

I arrived at the meeting, grabbed a cup of coffee, and sat in my usual location. As we greeted one another, I noticed a new attendee, a woman I had seen before. Christine humbly introduced herself in less than 25 words, which totally impressed me. Our deacon added that she was the author of a spiritual blog.

I was amazed how such a humble and quiet person could be a blogger. Intrigued, I asked for the name of her website. I discreetly looked it up on my cell phone and did a quick scan of the content and was consumed by a warmth of spirituality. Consumed is a soft word, as her writing embraced my mind and heart. I was drawn into a closeness to the words and pictures. I immediately subscribed to the distribution, an action I seldom do with anything online. After the meeting, I approached Christine. We talked for less than five minutes, yet I could sense how sincere and spiritually centered she was.

As I read more of her weekly posts, I became aware of her honesty and ability to share life happenings in a spiritual way. I realized she is totally in tune with the fact that life is made of ordinary things, and she is gifted in expressing this in her writing. Christine also captures images in photos that draw out spiritual insight without words. Through her photography, I have learned my life is a succession of visual snapshots and slices of time.

I am a Franciscan and love all of God's creatures, many of which are in my backyard. I am happy to feed and shelter them, even though they nest and dig in my flower beds and garden. Christine often posts pictures and stories of animals and nature, bringing creation to life. I read her words and end up forgetting about the flowers and garden, marveling at all God has given us to see and participate in. It is then I realize life is in scripture and scripture is in life. Christine sees scripture and life as one.

At one point, I wondered how she would be in a one-on-one conversation, since she was so humble and quiet. A movie at one of our linked parishes provided the setting for us to talk. As we conversed, Christine shared stories of God's presence in her life. Through our discussion, I came to know her as not only sincere and down to earth, but also a woman of mercy who has eyes to see others in need.

Christine routinely volunteers and serves meals to those in need. One evening as the soup kitchen closed, she was handed leftovers packaged in takeout containers to take home to her family (as a thank-you for serving). While walking to her car, she noticed an older couple drive into the parking lot hoping to be in time for the evening meal. Christine explained to them the soup kitchen had closed for the night. However, she could not let them leave empty-handed. She gave them her takeout meals and a bag of fresh vegetables. When I commended her for her selflessness, she humbly replied, "God has given me everything I need, and I want others to have what they need as well."

Once Christine noticed a woman in a car who was upset. She knocked on the window, introduced herself, and provided encouragement to the woman. Two strangers both felt led to pray with each other. Through offering hope to this woman, the random meeting began a long-term spiritual and personal relationship that has greatly touched the lives of both women.

Just looking at the stories Christine shares in this book is an indication of her heart for people and her love for God. She is God-inspired and God-centered. She sees and hears Him in every moment of her existence. Her prayers are the spirituality she lives and shares with our Lord, skillfully relating and referencing it to scripture. That is the central theme of her life and her writing, which she always hopes to use to inspire others.

I have had the pleasure of knowing and respectfully loving Christine in a personal and spiritual connection. From blog posts to conversations to photography, Christine has influenced and impacted my life. She inspires me to continuously see God everywhere – in everything and everyone. My final thoughts of Christine are expressed in some of her own words, "I hope the reader will see something in a different way or walk closer to the Lord through the words God has inspired and revealed to humankind."

May the reading of Christine's book be an inspirational journey of spirituality and love. Peace, love and blessings to you!

Lou Alfonsetti, Secular Franciscan Order
Endicott, New York

INTRODUCTION

God's presence is everywhere.

I have always felt a connection and closeness to the Lord but have found it hard to verbalize my thoughts. I discovered writing enables me to better understand what I feel and observe in the world around me. I started writing short poems before I was a teen. By my early 20s, I was penning short stories on how I saw God's presence in the world. I published some of my thoughts in our church newsletter and published booklets entitled "Treasured Verses" to share with family and friends.

Writing then took a 14-year hiatus as I focused on my growing family. In 2013, I was introduced to the Christian band, Third Day, and began following them on social media. This led to a "snowball effect." I started reading inspirational Christian blogs, which God used to rekindle my passion to write. I could relate to the blogs, and I felt led to see if this was something I could do. And, as they say, the rest is history.

My desire is to share Jesus through writing, which is inspired by the ordinary things in life. Being in tune with the "little" things reminds me how God's presence is illuminated in everything, everywhere, and every day. It is also a platform to share how I see God working in me, in others, in this beautiful world He created, and through the scriptures.

My prayer is that these thoughts will encourage you to see the world through a different lens or to walk closer to the Lord. As you take time to reflect on each story, may you be inspired with hope and light for your faith journey. Ultimately, I pray the Lord be glorified in my life and writings – God's presence illuminated.

Section 1

GOD'S PRESENCE ILLUMINATED IN CREATION

But ask the animals, and they will teach you, or the
birds of the air, and they will tell you;
or speak to the earth, and it will teach you, or
let the fish of the sea inform you.
Which of these does not know that the hand of the Lord has done this?
~ Job 12:7-9

The animals, the birds of the air, the earth, the seas, the fish, the heavens, the skies, the sun, the moon, day and night all proclaim the goodness of their Creator.

The Lord God made every inhabitant from the tiniest minnow to the giant elephant. The flowers of the fields and even the blades of grass are all part of God's creation.

Each of these living beings work together exactly as God made them; they, too, are His handiwork, just as we are.

God's presence illuminated in creation.

1

Encountering God

What are some different ways you encounter God's presence? Is it in the beauty of nature? Is it in the people you interact with like your family, coworkers, or people from church? Is it in inspiring music or books?

A friend and I took a trip to Virginia Beach during off-season to attend a nearby Christian concert. This was the first time either of us had visited this beautiful seaside town.

Our beachfront hotel was beside a horse corral, which was offering a horseback riding adventure along the coastline. I had never ridden a horse and was scared to attempt it, but my friend volunteered to go with me despite not really wanting to. We learned the corral recently moved to this location and the offer was only available for a few more weeks. It was a God thing for sure.

On the return trip to the corral, my horse and I strolled along the ocean. The other riders were a bit ahead. Though a little cool, the sun was high in the sky, beating down with its rays piercing my arms. Listening to the waves beat back and forth was soothing, and seeing the seagulls fly around, some with their snack in tow, caused my mind to wander back to the time of Jesus. I wondered what it was like as they spent most of their time fishing. I envisioned Jesus in a boat, calling His disciples to leave everything and follow Him.

It was a wonderful encounter reflecting on the beauty of nature and the power of Jesus in our lives. I was thankful for the opportunity to step out of my comfort zone and ride a horse on the beach. Encountering God was a special bonus.

How wonderful to experience God's presence even in the simple, little things. He is a great God and truly dwells in each of us and in all of nature. Seek Him and you will find Him.

Where can I go from your Spirit? Where can I flee from your presence?
If I go up to the heavens, you are there; if I make
my bed in the depths, you are there.
If I rise on the wings of the dawn, if I settle on the far side of the sea,
even there your hand will guide me, your right hand will hold me fast.
~ Psalm 139:7-10

2

Beach Time Reflections

How did God make and orchestrate all nature, all humanity, to be so perfect, so beautiful and to work so wonderfully together? Do you stop and wonder about the infinity of the ocean waters? How did God make all creation?

There is the sea, vast and spacious, teeming with creatures beyond number –
living things both large and small.
~ Psalm 104:25

One of my happy places is the ocean. Time away from the hustle and bustle, the routine of everyday life, and soaking up the beauty of the seashore is perfect. I am surrounded with God's love and peace.

What an awesome God we have; the One who made heaven, earth, the seas, little and big creatures of the ocean, the birds of the air, everything in this world. Even His most prized creation, you and me, are created in His image.

How does God make everything work together so perfectly day after day? How do each of these appear each day and night – the moon, sun, ocean waters, the earth revolving, the birds flying through the sky?

It is the Lord who provides the sun to light the day and the moon and
stars to light the night, and who stirs the sea into roaring waves. His
name is the Lord of Heaven's Armies, and this is what he says: "I am as
likely to reject my people Israel as I am to abolish the laws of nature."
~ Jeremiah 31:35-36 (NLT)

God provides for and oversees everything on this earth from the rising of the sun to the darkness of night to the raging seas. All creation is under His care, from the sky to you and me.

While at the ocean, do you, too, enjoy watching the continuity of the ocean waves flowing back and forth? As I watch the scene unfold before me, I am reminded of His love, grace and mercy that continually washes over our lives.

GOD'S LOVE

*I hear the tumult of the raging seas as your waves
and surging tides sweep over me.
But each day the Lord pours his unfailing love upon
me, and through each night I sing his songs,
praying to God who gives me life.*
~ Psalm 42:7-8 (NLT)

GOD'S GRACE

*Out of his fullness we have all received grace in place
of grace already given. For the law was given through
Moses; grace and truth came through Jesus Christ.*
~ John 1:16-17

GOD'S MERCY

His mercy flows in wave after wave on those who are in awe before him.
~ Luke 1:50 (MSG)

Another of God's amazing creations is the seagull. I am reminded of this Bible verse as I take in the view:

*Look at the birds.
They don't plant or harvest or store food in barns,
for your heavenly Father feeds them.
And aren't you far more valuable to him than they are?*

Christine M. Fisher

Can all your worries add a single moment to your life?
~ Matthew 6:26-27 (NLT)

Yes, the birds of the air are a good reminder, aren't they?

One time I was at the beach observing an awesome and unique sight. There were flocks of sparrows swarming in groups around the brush between the sidewalk and beach. They were even more of a reminder to be like the birds of the air.

Look at the ravens.
They don't plant or harvest or store food in barns, for God feeds them.
And you are far more valuable to him than any birds.
~ Luke 12:24 (NLT)

How very valuable we are to God. We need not worry, but rather we should trust Him more each day. God looks out for the birds of the air and provides for them moment by moment. He does the same for you and me.

I pray you remember how loved and valuable you are to the Creator of the world. The Creator who calms the seas and feeds the birds of the air cares even more deeply for you. He calms the storms in your life and provides all you need each day. Rejoice in Him.

When you go through deep waters, I will be with you.
When you go through rivers of difficulty, you will not drown.
When you walk through the fire of oppression, you will not be burned up;
the flames will not consume you.
~ Isaiah 43:2 (NLT)

3

The Sunrise

These words were inspired and quickly penned while I enjoyed a beautiful lake sunrise during a three-day retreat. I am blessed to have experienced this view, not only one, but two days.

Bright morning sunrise in the sky
reflecting upon the water
radiating out
just like you and me
radiating the Son in our lives.

Then appeared one bird
quickly followed by a second
and then a third
reminding me of the
Father, Son and Holy Spirit.

That third bird
lasting in the sky
the longest
reminding me of the
Holy Spirit's ever presence
in our lives.

There was an L-shaped cloud line
encompassing the sun
in the sky

Christine M. Fisher

reminding me of God's arms
always surrounding and
enveloping me.

After about fifteen minutes the cloud line
disappeared reminding me of the
Son's encompassing love and
inclusion of us all.

All different kinds of birds
were singing their songs of praise.
All in praise of their Creator
reminding me to do the same.

It was a grace filled moment experiencing
God's presence in creation and a definite
reminder for me of the "Sonrise" in our
hearts with Christ as the center.

The heavens declare the glory of God;
the skies proclaim the work of his hands.
~ Psalm 19:1

4

God's Masterpiece

As an artist sees an image and makes it come to life through some artistic media…
> creating a masterpiece,

As a musician writes lyrics and hears a melody to create beautiful music…
> creating a masterpiece,

As a writer uses words to express ideas through a book or simple writing…
> creating a masterpiece,

So, God envisioned and then created all His creations as His masterpieces. The masterpieces all have a purpose and work together to give Him praise and honor. Think about all the wonderful masterpieces God made…

> the sun and the moon,
> the earth and the heavens,
> the sky and the ocean waters,
> the plants and the trees,
> the birds and the animals,
> the mountains and the valleys.

And from those masterpieces, we get to behold…

> beautiful sunrises and sunsets,
> full moons to light our way,
> the bright stars illuminating the dark sky,
> the wonder of the crashing waves on the beach,
> the beautiful flowers in the meadow and the colorful leaves of the trees,
> the birds soaring through the air and making music for our ears,
> the majestic view of the mountains and the valleys.

Isn't God the ultimate artist creating such beauty for us where we can experience His love and power around us? If all those beautiful sights of creation were not enough, God then created His ultimate masterpiece...

you and me.

So God created man in his own image, in the image of God he created him; male and female he created them.
~ Genesis 1:27

Have you stopped to think how awesome it is that you are God's greatest masterpiece?

Let the power of that sink in...

You are created in His image...

You are truly a piece of our Master...

...That makes you a Masterpiece indeed.

Your hands shaped me and made me. Will you now turn and destroy me? Remember that you molded me like clay.
~ Job 10:8-9

5

Climbing Mountains

I climbed a mountain. Mt. Ampersand is over 3,300 feet high and is in the northeastern Adirondacks, west of the High Peaks in New York State. It was a nightmare because it had rained the day before, it was a pretty steep incline for a non-mountain climber, and the terrain was intense. During the hike, I was sure I was going to die, but somehow, I lived to tell about it. I was relieved when I made it safely down the mountain and was on level ground again (after slipping in the mud on the descent).

THIS EXPERIENCE MADE ME THINK ABOUT THE PARALLEL OF CLIMBING MOUNTAINS IN OUR LIVES.

We are lucky we do not know when the mountain climbs are coming. We cannot always see where the path is leading or how high the mountain is. If we knew what was ahead, we might try to avoid it and run the other way. Then we would never grow into the strong people God intended us to be.

Be strong and courageous. Do not be afraid or terrified because of them, for the Lord your God goes with you; he will never leave you nor forsake you.
~ Deuteronomy 31:6

IF WE TAKE ONE STEP AT A TIME OR ONE DAY AT A TIME, SLOWLY BUT SURELY, WE WILL MAKE IT TO THE TOP.

When climbing our mountain, we have no choice but to put one foot in front of the other, going step by step. If we stop to think about how far or where we are on our climb, we are bound to panic or lose our balance. We need only to look straight ahead and fix our eyes on Jesus.

Let us fix our eyes on Jesus, the author and perfecter of our faith,
who for the joy set before him endured the cross, scorning its
shame, and sat down at the right hand of the throne of God.
~ Hebrews 12:2

THROUGH THE ROUGH AND ROCKY TIMES, WE MUST GRAB ONTO THE LORD, SO WE DO NOT SLIP AND FALL.

In our mountain climb, we will encounter rocks and rough terrain where it will be necessary to hang onto something or someone to maintain our balance. We need to keep looking ahead, gather our strength and cling to the one true Rock, Jesus Christ.

The Lord is my rock, my fortress and my deliverer;
my God is my rock, in whom I take refuge.
He is my shield and the horn of my salvation, my stronghold.
~ Psalm 18:2

BEING PREPARED AT ALL TIMES IS ANOTHER IMPORTANT LESSON.

I found hiking the mountain in sneakers did not qualify as being well prepared. Hiking shoes would have made the trek more bearable. For our mountain climb, getting in a right relationship with God is one way to be prepared. Having true friends in the Lord and knowing the Word of God are definite necessities. They are our shield and the armor of God.

In addition to all this, take up the shield of faith, with which you can
extinguish all the flaming arrows of the evil one. Take the helmet of
salvation and the sword of the Spirit, which is the word of God.
~ Ephesians 6:16-17

THE VIEW FROM THE TOP WILL MAKE THE
HARD WORK WORTH THE EFFORT.

Have you experienced firsthand the beauty of the view after reaching the mountain's summit? The beauty can be breathtaking, and one cannot help but revel in the Creator of the Universe. Once we are at the summit of our mountain climb, we can thank the Lord for His help; we can enjoy the view, and we can praise Him for His goodness.

> *You will go out in joy and be led forth in peace; the*
> *mountains and the hills will burst into song before you,*
> *and all the trees of the field will clap their hands.*
> ~ Isaiah 55:12

Remember during the mountain times in your life, He is always with you, every step of the way.

> *…As I was with Moses, so I will be with you; I*
> *will never leave you nor forsake you.*
> ~ Joshua 1:5

6

Broken

A text from my friend said, "I was thinking of you while walking on the beach. There are a lot of broken shells, and I remember telling you how people are like broken shells. Broken but still beautiful." She added, "And the cool thing about these broken shells is they have all had an amazing journey." There is such great truth in these thoughts. Let's zero in on this phrase:

BROKEN BUT STILL BEAUTIFUL

On the beach, one finds broken shells galore. We know it is because of the journey of the shells. Consider a small seashell in such massive ocean waters. The shell is on a continual journey, minute by minute, day by day, floating, being tossed and turned, possibly crashing against boulders along the seashore. Perhaps parts of the seashell are left in different parts of the world. They all make it somewhere, somehow.

Our lives could represent those seashells. We are on an amazing journey that starts when we are born. Aren't we just one person in the big ocean of life surrounded by so many people and things? Aren't we on a continual, amazing journey, minute by minute, day by day? Throughout life, we get tossed around, sometimes even crashing into big boulders, the big issues that might try to break us. Don't we eventually make it to our ending point?

While reflecting on thoughts of "broken," I could not help but think of the one person who experienced ultimate brokenness so we might have everlasting life with God.

What an amazing journey Jesus had on this earth doing His Father's will. It was not always easy; people mocked Him, persecuted Him and some would not listen to Him. Jesus willingly suffered extreme brokenness when He endured His brutal death on the cross. This is the perfect example of how we can be *broken but still beautiful*. Yes, Jesus qualifies as the most beautiful person who graced this earth.

Through all the brokenness, we should remember...
>it is okay to be broken for a time.
>we are all broken.
>our brokenness may lead us to Christ.
>our brokenness will eventually end.
>God is still with us in our brokenness.
>God can mend our brokenness.
>our brokenness might help someone else on their journey.
>we can still reflect Jesus in our daily life.
>we can still trust God to get us through.
>our brokenness should be shared with others.
>we are still beautiful.

In Japanese culture, broken pottery is often repaired by filling it with gold, making it more beautiful and more valuable. What a great parallel for our lives—realizing our brokenness has made us more beautiful. We become better and stronger than we were before.

My friend also said, "God can use our broken pieces to make us more beautiful if we let Him. Give Him the pieces. *Broken things* can become *blessed things* if we allow God to do the mending."

He heals the brokenhearted and binds up their wounds.
~ Psalm 147:3

Christine M. Fisher

7

Our Journey of the Seasons

While thinking about the seasons,
    I couldn't help but think
how our life's journey is similar
    to the different seasons God created.

Sometimes, our walk with the Lord
    is like the springtime.
We see things in a new way
    and have so much hope.
We are like the budding flowers,
    emerging with renewed energy in full bloom.

Other times, our walk with the Lord
    is like the good ole summertime.
We rest peacefully knowing He is
    in control of our lives.
We enjoy the beauty of each day
    and live to the fullest.

At times, our walk with the Lord
    is like the fall time.
We see all the beautiful colors that
    surround us,
yet at the same time, we may grow
    tired and weary,
just as nature begins to slow down
    and hibernate.

Once in a while, our walk with the Lord
is like the wintertime –
kind of quiet and barren,
maybe even lonely.
The winter can be a time to grow within
and reflect on our journey.

In each season of our journey,
there are good days and bad days –
just like in the seasons, there are
cloudy days, stormy days,
and bright sunny days.

Each of the seasons has its own beauty
and specialness
just like the seasons
that God's children experience.

See. The winter is past; the rains are over and gone.
Flowers appear on the earth; the season of singing has come,
the cooing of doves is heard in our land.
The fig tree forms its early fruit; the blossoming vines spread their fragrance.
Arise, come, my darling; my beautiful one, come with me.
~ Song of Songs 2:11-13

8

Being Free

As I gazed into the bright, sunlit sky on a clear, cloudless day, I saw a bird soaring gently through the air. There was such beauty in the sight. God created the birds of the sky to soar with such freeness.

Wouldn't it be neat if we could be like the birds and spend our time singing and flying far throughout God's creation—just living moment by moment?

As I continued to think about the birds, I couldn't help but think maybe God was showing me this bird to remind me to be more like them…

> do not worry about tomorrow.
> simply live one moment at a time.
> rest in His love and care.

He will be our strength and provide all we need when we need it.

As we grow more and more in faith and trust, we will be more like the birds—our spirits will soar freely with Him—free of the tensions and worries of this world.

Look at the birds of the air; they do not sow or reap or store away in barns,
and yet your heavenly Father feeds them. Are you
not much more valuable than they?
Who of you by worrying can add a single hour to his life?
~ Matthew 6:26-27

9

The Ocean Reminder

I stood in the ocean, peering into the blue-green water with the soft, white sand beneath my feet. It took days before I observed the fish swimming past my legs. They never brushed against me, so I did not realize they were there. The day I noticed them, a yellow and black striped fish swam past followed by two sunfish. Later in the week, there were schools of fish finding their way in the water. These sightings intrigued me to think more about God and His infinite vastness, about the life that takes place in the ocean waters without us realizing it. Yes, from the whales to dolphins, to starfish, to jellyfish, to coral reefs, to rocks, to seahorses. There is a whole world in the ocean waters, which often goes unnoticed by us.

Isn't that a great reminder of how God is always at work in this world? He makes the ocean waters a working world in and of itself; the same goes for all nature; the trees and plants that continually change and evolve; the wild animals of the world which roam about and populate.

Isn't that a great reminder of how God is always at work in our lives orchestrating events and moments? We do not physically see Him on this earth, yet He is always present; creating, sustaining and working on our behalf.

Have you seen Him working in every aspect of your life? How amazing to think He is always working everything out for us.

Think about the friend you saw when you were walking on the trail. Seeing them reminded you to say a prayer asking the Lord to bless them in whatever their need may be.

Think about the timing of events when you took a leap of faith to message someone you had not seen in a long time. With reaching out, you learned about a struggle they were walking through and were able to pray for them.

Think about the person who surprised you with flowers when you needed a little encouragement.

Yes, God is always at work in this world—from the ocean waters, to the highest mountain, to the big and small details of our lives.

"Am I only a God nearby," declares the Lord, "and not a God far away?
Who can hide in secret places so that I cannot see them?" declares the Lord.
"Do not I fill heaven and earth?" declares the Lord.
~ Jeremiah 23:23-24 (NLT)

10

Signs of His Love

I was engulfed in the Lord's presence one day while standing at the gravesites of my grandparents, great-aunt and great-uncle…
> all nature was just "being"
> so bright and beautiful.

Up in the sky floated big, puffy, cotton-like clouds…
> giving me a sense of awesomeness
> and wonder.

Behind the clouds, the sky was a beautiful shade of blue
so bright and cheerful…
> reminding me of crystal clear blue water
> maybe even the Crystal Sea in heaven.

The big round hills in the distance were bearing trees with their green leaves in many shades. I am always amazed at the numerous trees on the hills and the beauty they bring though no one takes care of them…
> reminding me how God takes care of all His creation.

The pinecone-shaped trees were standing tall with such a deep green color, so perfectly shaped…
> reminding me how the Lord prunes every one of us to
> mold and shape us into His own image.

Many types of flowers dotted the scene, some real, some artificial. I thought of the people who brought them to honor their family and friends…
> reminding me the flowers were brought in love, reflecting
> a little of ourselves, in the many types and colors.

Christine M. Fisher

The birds filled the air with praise, singing their songs and chirping constantly, a sign of beauty...

> reminding me the Lord takes care of even the littlest bird—how much more He takes care of us.

The earth was illuminated so brightly by the sun, its heat penetrated deep into my body...

> reminding me of God's warming love for each of us.

To top off this beauty, there was a gentle, warm breeze blowing...

> reminding me of the Holy Spirit, God's gift to guide and help us every day.

We are truly surrounded by signs of His love in...

> nature
> animals
> plants
> flowers
> and the people God puts in our path.

Take time to see the signs of His love and share that love with all you meet. Give thanks and praise Him continually for His goodness.

The heavens declare the glory of God; the skies
proclaim the work of His hands.
Day after day they pour forth speech; night
after night they display knowledge.
There is no speech or language where their voice is not heard.
Their voice goes out into all the earth, their words to the ends of the world.
~ Psalm 19:1-4

11

Our Awesome God

As I looked at the vastness of this earth while cruising 37,000 feet in an airplane, I was overwhelmed with this thought: Our God is so awesome— He has more knowledge, wisdom and power than all the people in this world put together.

Man has used his brain and technology to do so much over the years. Man has the knowledge to design and make airplanes that can transport people halfway across the world. *Yet, man does not have the power to design and create the space the plane travels through.*

Man can build computers that produce mathematical calculations in hundredths of a second that would take days to do using hand calculations. *But man can't control or calculate the length of his life span on earth.*

Man has the wisdom to perform delicate brain surgery, and in most cases, the patient recovers and leads a "normal" life. *Yet, man does not have the ability to create a human brain or revive it once dead.*

As I continued to reflect on the vastness of this earth and our awesome God who created everything, there was one thought that really amazed me.

Though I am such a little part of this vast earth, with all its surroundings, all the animals and the billions of people, our awesome God has the capacity to know, love and care for me. How everything, even my life, can be under His control is awesome and mind-boggling.

Our God is so awesome. He does the same for you. He knows, loves, and cares for you!

Christine M. Fisher

*When I consider your heavens, the work of your
fingers, the moon and the stars,
which you have set in place, what is man that you are mindful of him,
the son of man that you care for him?*
~ Psalm 8:3-4

12

Let Go and Let God

The trees are about to let us know how lovely it is to let things go.

For those who live in the parts of the world that experience the changes of the four seasons, you can appreciate the above quote. As the cool, crisp weather returns for another fall season, the leaves on the trees turn from their green summer color to vibrant yellows, oranges, or reds before letting go. Aren't the fall tree colors a beautiful sight? If the trees did not go through the seasonal changes, we might not see the loveliness in letting go.

Have you thought about that same principle in relation to life? Do you see the loveliness in letting go? Try to answer these two questions encompassing both worldly and spiritual realms:

> What are some things you try to control that you might need to let go?

> What are some different things you need to let go so you can experience loveliness?

Here are a few things to consider letting go…
control of your life.
the way others respond to you.
your children's lives.
toxic relationships.
the path you think your life should go.
fear that overtakes your life.
pride that gets in the way of being humble.
sin that keeps you from God.

your own will without praying for guidance.

worry that cripples you from moving forward.

anger that overtakes you.

Life is about letting go. Isn't this more apparent, especially as we age?

If we have children, we watch them get to the point where they are ready to leave the nest.

We don't need as many things.

Participating in sports, for either our self or family members eventually ends.

We lose contact with school friends and coworkers.

As relatives age, we let them go to their eternal reward.

We can let go because we give God control. Who is really in charge of your life? I hope you can answer with a resounding, "God is in control!" We can trust God because...

HE HAS SUCH GREAT LOVE FOR US.
*God showed how much he loved us by sending
his one and only Son into the world
so that we might have eternal life through him.*
~ 1 John 4:9 (NLT)

HE IS OUR FATHER WHO WANTS ONLY
THE BEST FOR US, HIS CHILDREN.
*See what great love the Father has lavished on us,
that we should be called children of God.
And that is what we are. The reason the world does
not know us is that it did not know him.*
~ 1 John 3:1

HE WORKS EVERYTHING OUT FOR OUR GOOD.
And we know that God causes everything to work together for the good
of those who love God and are called according to his purpose for them.
~ Romans 8:28 (NLT)

HE PROVIDES THE PEACE THAT
SURPASSES ALL UNDERSTANDING.
Then you will experience God's peace, which
exceeds anything we can understand.
His peace will guard your hearts and minds as you live in Christ Jesus.
~ Philippians 4:7 (NLT)

HE IS ALWAYS WITH US, THROUGH
THE THICK AND THIN.
This is my command—be strong and courageous.
Do not be afraid or discouraged.
For the Lord your God is with you wherever you go.
~ Joshua 1:9 (NLT)

Here is another quote to consider:

"We stress ourselves out because we put ourselves
where God is supposed to be."
~ Pastor Louis, Kingdom Revival Church

Doesn't this quote make sense? Think about the phrase, "Let go and let God." Ask God to reveal times when you need to let go and trust Him. Life is about change and surrendering, let go and let God. May it be an encouragement to remember change is good. God made everything on this earth to change...the only thing that never changes is God Himself.

Commit to the Lord whatever you do, and he will establish your plans.
~ Proverbs 16:3

13

God's Creations

What an amazing Creator we have. God created every living creature in this world, from the littlest sea creature and the smallest plant to the huge elephant, and even you and me. Every creature God created is different and unique. I pondered that thought while visiting a local zoo with my son.

While at the zoo...

I loved seeing how the snow leopard's tail was as long as its whole body.

I noticed how the black toed penguins and the river otters, my son's favorite, are so cute. In fact, they are almost as cute and cuddly as the panda bear, my favorite.

Watching the gray and red wolves move around was somewhat eerie, but it was nice to see the differences between them. The red wolf is longer legged and is smaller than the gray wolf.

I never realized the smallness of the arctic fox.

God graced the earth with unique animals to populate our beautiful world. While reflecting on the animals at the zoo, I was in awe with thinking how God then made humans. Just as all the animals, plants, and birds are unique and special in their own way, so are humans.

God created everything and everyone to do His will. All praise and honor belong to Him for all His creation. We humans have the greatest honor—being made in His image.

But ask the animals, and they will teach you, or the birds of the air, and they will tell you; or speak to the earth, and it will teach you, or let the fish of the sea inform you. Which of all these does not know that the hand of the Lord has done this? In his hand is the life of every creature and the breath of all mankind.

~ Job 12:7-10

Christine M. Fisher

14

The Beauty of the Sun

When the sun shines so gloriously, are you mesmerized by the sight?

The beauty of the sun reminds me of the presence of the SON in our lives.
How I love to see...

    the beautiful sunrise.

    the sun shining brightly in the sky during the day.

    the serene sunset to close out the day.

I am blessed to see the sun shining forth...

    over the ocean waters.

    peeking through the awesome cloud formations.

    over the mountains and hills.

    over the horizon.

    through the tall, sturdy trees.

The sun is mesmerizing to me because...

    it lights up the whole sky and shines down on the earth.

    it radiates amazing streaks of rays.

    of the different colors it uses to paint the sky—sometimes reds, pinks, and purples.

    of seeing how the sun rises and sets on the same horizon.

Things the shining sun reminds me...

    we are enveloped in the Son's presence all day, every day.

    of the love and peace the Son grants.

    of the mercies of the Lord which are new every day.

    how the Son needs to shine and radiate through us.

    of the beauty of the world the Lord created.

of the beauty of all God's children.

how the Son fills our lives.

how the Son is everywhere.

how the Son starts as a little glow in our hearts and grows to a huge light.

how the Son is always present in our lives.

From the rising of the sun to the place where it sets,
the name of the Lord is to be praised.
~ Psalm 113:3

Christine M. Fisher

15

The Fire

While viewing a campfire at night, I was fascinated by the sight of it continuously burning. This reminded me of our relationship with the Lord. I imagined God being the spark that comes when we first start the fire, and then grows into a big, glowing fire, if we do the "right" things.

For a fire to exist, we must first consciously gather the proper materials and start the fire. So it is in our relationship with God. We must first decide we are ready to fan into existence our commitment to the Lord. We must prepare ourselves by repenting and seeking Him with our heart.

In order to get and keep the fire burning, we must continually add more logs. How we do this determines how brightly the fire burns. The same principles work to show how brightly the Lord shines through our life. If we use a good, long burning log, the spark turns into a great, hot flame. If we use a sappy log, the fire will not burn, it will only smolder and smoke. Soon, it will die out.

The choices are parallel in our relationship with God. If we read and study His word and seek His presence in our lives (good wood), our fire will burn brightly. If we are too busy for the Lord and do not seek Him daily (bad wood), our fire will soon die out.

Be honest. Think about how brightly your fire is burning. Can other people see a continuously blazing fire shining for the Lord?

I have come to bring fire on the earth, and how
I wish it were already kindled.
~ Luke 12:49

16

Living Waters

Spending time near bodies of water, like the ocean, renews my spirit by revealing God's love to me.

Doesn't the ocean appear to be never ending?
> Just like God's love for us. No matter what, His love for us never ends.

What about the rough ocean waves?
> Through the rough patches in our lives, God rides out the storm with us.

Are you fascinated by watching the tide continually ebb and flow?
> God's love continually washes over us too.

Have you seen the big waves come along engulfing whatever is in its way?
> God's love is always ready to embrace us, even when we stray from Him.

What about when the ocean waters are still and calm?
> It is the peace we find in God's loving arms.

It is engaging to watch the interactions of people on the beach. I watched a young mother holding her six-month-old baby. She wrapped her arms around the baby, holding him tightly as the waves washed over them. It reminded me how God embraces us, keeping us safe during life's storms that try to shake us.

The seagulls soaring in the sky reminded me of the Holy Spirit who is ready to help us soar to new heights. Observing a seagull or two just sitting on top of the ocean water, coasting with the waves, reminded me how we need to coast along with the Lord leading us.

I am thankful for the living waters we see in this world that help us make the connection with Jesus, the true living water, who refreshes, renews, and revitalizes us.

> *On the last and greatest day of the festival, Jesus stood and said*
> *in a loud voice, "Let anyone who is thirsty come to me and drink.*
> *Whoever believes in me, as Scripture has said, rivers of living water*
> *will flow from within them." By this he meant the Spirit, whom*
> *those who believed in him were later to receive. Up to that time the*
> *Spirit had not been given, since Jesus had not yet been glorified.*
> ~ John 7:37-39

17

Bouquet

Do you enjoy looking at a bouquet of flowers, in awe of the beauty? There may be many different colors, sizes, shapes, and types of flowers. Do you notice how each is unique and beautiful in its own way? Maybe you like the color of one, or maybe a type of flower is your favorite and brings back a special memory. Isn't that just like the people in your life?

We are all different. We come in different colors, sizes, and shapes. We bring different things to life. We have different gifts to share with one another. When we work together, despite our differences, we are a beautiful representation of God's handiwork. This is like the beauty reflected in a variety of flowers brought together.

At first, we may notice some of the flowers are just starting to bud but after a few days, the flowers open and come to full bloom. Taking time to listen to others and share God's love is like the flowers reaching their full bloom state. When we care for others, we are sprouting, growing nice and tall, and opening to reflect God's mercy and goodness to those around us. If God's love does not fill our lives, we are more like the poor, wilting flowers. We won't survive long.

To preserve the bouquet of flowers for the longest time, they need...
> fresh water daily,
> the sun,
> and maybe even a little pruning.

Isn't that just like us?

Christine M. Fisher

Daily, we need…

> God's word to refresh us.
>
> The "Son" reflected through our lives to others.
>
> To receive the "Son" from others into our lives.

Sometimes, we need a little "pruning" or correction to get us back on the path of following Him. It may be painful, but He is always ready to love and guide us back to Him. He is our Loving Father.

For you have been born again, not of perishable seed, but of imperishable, through the living and enduring word of God. For "All men are like grass, and all their glory is like the flowers of the field; the grass withers and the flowers fall, but the word of the Lord stands forever." And this is the word that was preached to you.
~ 1 Peter 1:23-25

18

Sun Reflections

One of my favorite things has always been watching the setting of the sun. On a beach trip, I decided to experience a sunrise. The first morning the horizon was clear, so I was able to observe the sunrise from the hotel balcony. A feeling of expectation came over me as I waited for the display of God's beautiful masterpiece to rise.

The whole day was ahead of me waiting to see what special blessings it held…
>   The ways I could praise Him from morning till night.
>   Seeing how each interaction would be intricately woven in God's master plan.
>   Finding out whose life I could touch and how He would use others to touch my life.

It was quiet and still as I first observed the skyline display the magnificent colors. Then the sun peeked out little by little, as it moved up the horizon and far into the sky, spreading to reflect and glisten on the ocean waters. This verse came to mind:

> *From the rising of the sun to the place where it sets,*
> *the name of the Lord is to be praised.*
> ~ Psalm 113:3

What a beautiful and perfect verse to start the day. Yes, we need to praise His name from the rising of the sun until it sets, and even during the night.

The second day, I was a little disappointed to see a band of clouds along the horizon, which made me think of how God, the Light, is with us even

Christine M. Fisher

during the dark, cloudy times. Even more powerful is the way light always shines through the darkness. Yes, light wins. The band of clouds eventually cleared the sky and I saw another glorious sunrise.

Have you noticed how, after the sun rises above the ocean, it can be seen glistening and spreading to larger areas on the waters? Isn't that like Christ in us? Don't we radiate His Light to others, spreading to more and more people?

That evening, the sunset was the exact same way. The sun had to pass through darker clouds before reaching the horizon. Before setting, it appeared gloriously in the sky, reminding me how light always triumphs over darkness.

I pray that your life may reflect the different facets of the sun.
Each day may you rise to shine His beauty
that is within you to this world.
Shine through the darkness, the clouds in this world,
to shine His Light.
Wait patiently in expectation of how the Lord
will use you to bless others' lives.
Be excited to see how He uses people to
encourage your faith journey each day.
Take time to be still in His presence.
May your life radiate His love, goodness, grace, and mercy.
May Christ in you spread to all you encounter.

Soak up the Son's peace. Reflect the Son's radiance to all. Praise the Lord in everything, from the rising of the sun to its setting, and during the night. When evening comes, refresh your body and soul by spending time resting with the Son.

Be still and know that I am God. I will be exalted among the nations,
I will be exalted in the earth.
~ Psalm 46:10 (ESV)

19

The Mighty Mountains

Gazing upon the mighty mountains in Estes Park, Colorado was truly a breathtaking, captivating sight, like a little piece of heaven on earth. Viewing this spectacular beauty of nature that God, in His infinite providence, created was such a peaceful experience. Sitting with the view of the mountains, so great and majestic, with the sun's radiance beaming on me and the wind blowing across my face, I experienced the Trinity–Father (the mountain), Son (the Sun), and Holy Spirit (the wind).

This was my first experience soaking in the proximity of the mighty mountains. I kept gravitating between the view of the majestic mountains, some with patches of fresh June snow, and a cross in the foreground. Observing these mammoth creations, one cannot help but know that God's love reaches far beyond.

The Mighty Mountains made me reflect more about God.

- Majestic is our God; His majesty is even greater than the tallest mountain.
- In our lives, God is in charge of all our mountains.
- Goodness and unconditional love are what our God has for us.
- How God is greater than the biggest, steepest, roughest mountain in our life.
- The heavens, earth, stars, seas, mountains and plains are all made by our great God.
- You can never outdo our God in power.

Christine M. Fisher

- Mighty in power is our God.
- Our God made us even more beautiful than the mountains.
- Undeniably, God's presence can be felt and seen in the mountains.
- Need to be still and know that He is God of all.
- The greatest of all God's creation is you and I.
- Awe-struck of all God's wonderful provisions in our life.
- Infinite is God's grace and mercy that He bestows on us, His children.
- Near in Spirit is our God.
- Someday, we will see our mighty and majestic God face to face.

Your righteousness is like the mighty mountains,
your justice like the ocean depths.
You care for people and animals alike, O Lord.
~ Psalm 36:6 (NLT)

20

The Message of the Tree

In the Bible, Jesus shares parables about animals and nature to help us think about our human nature and our relationship with Him. Consider a simple, big old tree—even it can speak to us about our personal relationship with Jesus Christ.

Envision the big, sturdy trunk of a tree, representing Jesus, the firm and solid foundation. From the trunk grow many branches, you and me, which eventually produce beautiful colorful leaves. Each leaf, each of us, reflects the beauty of its source, Jesus, to all who see them.

Consider how the leaves and branches get their nutrition from the roots and trunk in order to grow. As Christians, our main source, Jesus and scripture, are our major supply of growth. Without this life-giving supply from the roots and trunk, the branches could not survive.

Occasionally, a branch or two gets out of hand and grows the wrong way. When this happens, the branch may need pruning to shape it. Don't we sometimes get that way too?

At times, storms come along, shaking the branches and leaves, but they survive if their grip is tight to the source, the trunk. We, too, will survive the storms and trials of life if our grip is tight to our source, Jesus. The storms eventually pass away, and all will be calm again.

So then, just as you received Christ Jesus as Lord, continue to live your lives in him, rooted and built up by him, strengthened in the faith as you were taught, and overflowing with thankfulness.
~ Colossians 2:6-7

Christine M. Fisher

21

Footprints

As a friend and I walked along the shore, it was soothing to watch tractors comb the beach, giving a fresh canvas for our footprints. Though the combing gave it a rough appearance, the sand was soft and smooth. We were reminded of the poem, "Footprints in the Sand," which paints the picture of Jesus walking beside us, and when the journey gets rough, He often carries us.

Here are a few things to ponder.

> As we walk each day, God walks alongside us, though we do not physically see Him.
>
> His footprints are there even when we turn our back on Him. Yes, He is our Good Father who is still walking with us, allowing us to exercise our free will.
>
> Sometimes we stumble and fall. What does God do? He gently picks us up, brushes off the sand and dirt, and sets us back on track, walking beside us every step of the way.
>
> When the path gets rough and we think we cannot go on, He scoops us up and carries us, one step at a time.

Try to be more aware of God walking alongside you and gathering you in His loving arms when the going gets rough. He loves and cares deeply for you. Embrace His outstretched arms.

And you saw how the Lord your God cared for you all along the way as you traveled through the wilderness, just as a father cares for his child. Now he has brought you to this place.
~ Deuteronomy 1:31 (NLT)

22

The Sun

The "SUN" is a shining reminder of Jesus, the "SON" in our life.

If you have ever seen the sun rise
from behind the hills and mountains,
you may have been blessed
by the sparkling red and yellow rays that fill the sky.

Just gazing on this beautiful sight
reminds us how much beauty is in creation—
both inanimate and living,
there is a breathtaking awesomeness in the sight.

So may all your enemies perish, O Lord.
But may they who love you be like the sun when it rises in its strength.
Then the land had peace forty years.
- Judges 5:31

During the day, see the sun brighten the earth
and penetrate so deeply and warmly.
I enjoy being immersed in the warmth of the sun
as its rays are radiating so intensely.

A sign and symbol of all the love God gives us
through His "Son," Jesus.
Jesus' love for us is deeply rooted in us
and rises to brighten the lives of others.

For the Lord God is a sun and shield; the Lord bestows favor and honor;
no good thing does he withhold from those whose walk is blameless.
~ Psalm 84:11

In the evening, see the sun setting over the ocean waters–
such a tranquil and serene view.
This sight restores our soul
letting us know God is in control,
and He is filling us with His peace and love.

From the rising of the sun to the place where it sets,
the name of the Lord is to be praised.
~ Psalm 113:3

Christine M. Fisher

23

God's Presence

We often limit ourselves to thinking God's presence is only found in us, so that is the only way we can share Him with others. Have you considered how God created everything in the world before creating humans? God's presence can be found in all creation.

Have you noticed God's presence in...
>   the evening sunset,
>   the puffy, white clouds,
>   the crystal, clear water,
>   the hot, sparkling afternoon sun?

>   the colorful wildflowers,
>   the picturesque path in the woods,
>   the birds chirping away,
>   the bright fall foliage?

>   the quietness of the sparkling snow,
>   the ice and snow on the river,
>   the brilliant rainbow in the sky,
>   the rolling hills and mountains?

If you take a minute to look, you will find the presence of the Lord in these places too. All creation shares in revealing God's presence and praising Him.

You will go out in joy and be led in peace;
the mountains and hills will burst into song before you,
and all the trees of the field will clap their hands.
~ Isaiah 55:12

Section 2

GOD'S PRESENCE ILLUMINATED IN SCRIPTURE

Your word, O Lord, is eternal; it stands firm in the heavens.
Your word is a lamp to my feet and a light for my path.
~ Psalm 119:89, 105

God knew. He knew that once He breathed life into Adam, Man would need help. He knew our first parents, Adam and Eve, would eat from the forbidden tree of life. He knew all humans would need a book to guide their lives.

Through God's word we learn about God's characteristics and how to live. We also learn how much God loves us. He demonstrated His love by sending His only Son, Jesus, to be born on earth and then die to set us free from our sin.

God's word has stood the test of time. It was true and relevant more than 2,000 years ago and it still holds true. God's word stands forever, it is eternal. God's word is a lamp showing the path we need to follow and indeed, it is living and active.

God's presence illuminated in scripture.

24

Lessons from the Ark

What lessons can we apply to our lives from the story of Noah and the ark? The whole story can be found in Genesis 6 through Genesis 9:17. Here are some key verses and parallels from the story to think about in relation to our lives.

> *Noah was a righteous man, blameless among the*
> *people of his time, and he walked with God.*
> ~ Genesis 6:9

Righteous means honoring God, following Him in all we do. If we are in positions of power and authority, our righteousness should bless, not exploit. Do you suppose this serves as a reminder to live righteously, loving God first and then loving others as ourselves?

> *Noah did everything just as God commanded him.*
> ~ Genesis 6:22

This refers to the building of the ark with all the measurements, and bringing the exact people, animals, living creatures, and kinds of food into the ark, as commanded by God.

> *And Noah did all that the Lord commanded him.*
> ~ Genesis 7:5

This was in reference to the actual time the Lord told Noah to go into the ark, along with the clean and unclean animals. Do you suppose the two verses above serve as a reminder to obey God when we hear His voice and not to harden our hearts against Him?

The animals going in were male and female of every
living thing, as God had commanded Noah.
Then the Lord shut him in.
~ Genesis 7:16

Isn't it incredible to think that God was so in control, He shut the door of the ark when the time was right? Do you suppose this serves as a reminder to know God does things in His perfect timing? When God shuts the door, we know it is the right time, and we are safe with Him.

For forty days the flood kept coming on the
earth, and as the waters increased,
they lifted the ark high above the earth. The waters
rose and increased greatly on the earth,
and the ark floated on the surface of the water.
~ Genesis 7:17-18

Can you visualize the amount of water on the earth after forty days and nights of continual rain, along with a single ark being tossed and turned all over creation? Do you suppose this serves as a reminder to ride out the storms of life and trust the unknown to our God? Just as the ark was a protection for Noah and his family, God is our ark.

But God remembered Noah and all the wild animals
and the livestock that were with him in the ark,
and he sent a wind over the earth, and the waters receded.
~ Genesis 8:1

What was on God's mind? He was considering Noah and every living creature on the ark. Aren't we always on God's mind too? Doesn't it show us how much God cares for His creation? Do you think this serves as a reminder that just as God sent a wind over the earth and the water receded,

He cares for us? The wind is symbolic of the Holy Spirit that comes over us, working things out in our life and bringing us peace.

After forty days, Noah opened the window he had made in the ark.
~ Genesis 8:6

I learned there were probably a series of windows placed in the ark within 18 inches of the roof. Do you suppose this serves as a reminder to look up to God, to trust Him, and to see our value in Him, not from the things or people around us? We are to look up, not around or even within.

By the first day of the first month of Noah's six hundred and first year, the water had dried up from the earth. Noah then removed the covering from the ark and saw that the surface of the ground was dry.
~ Genesis 8:13

Noah and all the creatures were in the ark for more than one year. I wonder what they did that whole time. Do you suppose this serves as a reminder to take time to rest and sit in the presence of God? When we rest, we can be filled with God's grace and the peace only He can give—a peace beyond all understanding.

And God said, "This is the sign of the covenant I am making between me and you and every living creature with you, a covenant for all generations to come: I have set my rainbow in the clouds, and it will be the sign of the covenant between me and the earth."
~ Genesis 9:12-13

Though rain was mentioned earlier in Genesis, this is the first time the rainbow is mentioned, which was now a symbol of God's covenant for all generations to come. Do you suppose this serves as a reminder to always have hope in our lives? Ultimately, things will work out because God reigns over all. What really matters is spending eternity with our God and Savior.

I pray that God, the source of hope, will fill you completely with joy and peace because you trust in him. Then you will overflow with confident hope through the power of the Holy Spirit.
~ Romans 15:13 (NLT)

25

The True Light

The true light that gives light to every man was coming into the world.
~ John 1:9

Who is the true light John speaks of coming into the world? Jesus. How do we know Jesus is the true light?

> *When Jesus spoke again to the people, he said, "I am the*
> *light of the world. Whoever follows me will never walk*
> *in darkness, but will have the light of life."*
> ~ John 8:12

Jesus directly says He is the light and if we follow Him, we do not have to live in darkness, nor do we have to let Satan control us. Jesus is the true light who gives light to every man. This means Jesus gives light to you and me. The light started when Jesus came into the world, born a baby. It is our responsibility and privilege to receive His light into our hearts when we accept Jesus as our Lord and Savior. We are then entrusted with that same light and need to share His light with all we meet.

What does Jesus say about this light He gives us?

> *You are the light of the world. A city on a hill cannot be hidden.*
> *Neither do people light a lamp and put it under a bowl. Instead*
> *they put it on its stand, and it gives light to everyone in the house.*
> *In the same way, let your light shine before men, that they may*
> *see your good deeds and praise your Father in heaven.*
> ~ Matthew 5:14-16

We are now the light of this world.

Our light needs to shine for Him for all to see.

We are not to hide our light.

We are to do good with our light.

Our light will reflect praise back to our Father.

Do all things without grumbling or disputing, that
you may be blameless and innocent,
children of God without blemish in the midst
of a crooked and twisted generation,
among whom you shine as lights in the world, holding fast to the word of life,
so that in the day of Christ I may be proud that I
did not run in vain or labor in vain.
~ Philippians 2:14-16 (ESV)

Do not complain.

Do not argue.

Be wholeheartedly devoted to God's will.

Be honest and sincere.

Hold fast to God's Word.

Live every moment for the Lord.

What are some practical ways we can shine our light daily?

Read and apply scripture.

Be careful of what we watch on television and the music we listen to.

Pray continually throughout the day.

Bring the light to others through an encouraging word.

Check on a shut-in or neighbor who is lonely.

Sincerely care about those we meet.

Encourage our friends and even our pastor.

Guard our mouth and speak positive, edifying words to others.

Share the treasure the Lord has provided us.

Seek the unique gift the Lord has given us and use it for His glory.

May the light of Jesus we have received and been entrusted with, shatter the darkness of this world, and point all we meet to Jesus, the True Light of the world. Amen.

For God, who said, "Let light shine out of darkness," made his light to shine in our hearts to give us the light of the knowledge of the glory of God in the face of Christ.
~ 2 Corinthians 4:6

26

Hope

Have you considered what a vital role *hope* plays in our lives? There is the world's hope and there is biblical hope. We often say to someone, "I hope you have a nice day," or "I sure hope your test for a health issue comes back negative." Using the word hope in this way seems to mean we desire or strongly wish something good will occur and produce a favorable outcome. This is the worldly view of hope; hope that is founded in uncertainty or without strong assurance.

Let's look at scripture relating to biblical *hope*.

> *Three things will last forever - faith, hope, and*
> *love - and the greatest of these is love.*
> ~ 1 Corinthians 13:13 (NLT)

Hope must be more than a desire or wish if it is something that will last forever.

> *"The Lord is my portion," says my soul, "therefore I will hope in him."*
> ~ Lamentations 3:24 (ESV)

Hope is based on the Lord: someone concrete and true. Hope is as strong and trustworthy as an anchor; something concrete.

> *...Therefore, we who have fled to him for refuge can have great*
> *confidence as we hold to the hope that lies before us. This*
> *hope is a strong and trustworthy anchor for our souls.*
> *It leads us through the curtain into God's inner*
> *sanctuary. Jesus has already gone in there for us.*

Christine M. Fisher

He has become our eternal High Priest in the order of Melchizedek.
~ Hebrews 6:18-20 (NLT)

What does biblical *hope* look like?

> Confident expectation – not wishful thinking.
> Definite assurance – not lacking faith.
> Moral certainty – not necessarily logical.

Remember…this hope is a strong and trustworthy anchor for our souls. Hebrews 6:18-20 creates a vivid image of our hope. Consider what an anchor does for a ship. It connects a vessel to a body of water preventing the vessel from drifting, whether due to wind or the water's current. Isn't that just like hope connecting us to God, preventing us from drifting when the storms of life come upon us?

Remember this acrostic for the word HOPE….

> Heaven's ultimate
> Outpouring of the
> Promises from our
> Eternal Savior.

Be encouraged today to live out the biblical *hope* we have available to us in Christ.

> *"For I know the plans I have for you,"* declares the Lord,
> *"plans to prosper you and not to harm you,*
> *plans to give you hope and a future."*
> ~ Jeremiah 29:11

27

Love

Unity of the body of Christ is taught in 1 Corinthians 12. We all have different spiritual gifts God has given to build up and share with one another. We are one body in Christ, yet the body is comprised of many parts. Each member needs to do their part, using their spiritual gifts to edify the body of Christ.

Do you know what else Paul is saying? We are all equal. No person or gift is greater than another. Paul writes about living in a more "excellent" way. What is that way? Living in love. All the spiritual gifts we have and all we do for the body of Christ needs to be done with and through love. It all means nothing unless love is our motivation (1 Corinthians 12:31-13:13).

Consider these two sets of Bible verses. Then we will use them to dust off cobwebs as we apply a math concept for deeper understanding.

In the beginning was the Word, and the Word
was with God, and the Word was God.
He was with God in the beginning.
Through him all things were made;
without him nothing was made that has been made.
~ John 1:1-3

I and the Father are one.
~ John 10:30

These two verses prove that God and Jesus are two but really one— unified. GOD = JESUS

We know how much God loves us, and we have put our trust in his love.
God is love, and all who live in love live in God, and God lives in them.
~ 1 John 4:16 (NLT)

But anyone who does not love does not know God, for God is love.
~ 1 John 4:8 (NLT)

Both verses define God as love.
GOD = LOVE

Let's apply the mathematical formula of a = b and a = c then we know
b = c. When we plug our formula with names, we get:

GOD = JESUS
GOD = LOVE

Then we know:
JESUS = LOVE

Let's look at the original 1 Corinthians passage substituting *Jesus* for the
word *love*.

> *Brothers and sisters:*
> *Strive eagerly for the greatest spiritual gifts.*
> *But I shall show you a still more excellent way.*
> *If I speak in human and angelic tongues, but do not have JESUS,*
> *I am a resounding gong or a clashing cymbal.*
> *And if I have the gift of prophecy, and comprehend all mysteries and*
> *all knowledge;*
> *if I have all faith so as to move mountains, but do not have JESUS,*
> *I am nothing.*
> *If I give away everything I own, and if I hand my body over so that*
> *I may boast,*
> *but do not have JESUS, I gain nothing.*

JESUS is patient, JESUS is kind. JESUS is not jealous, JESUS is not pompous.

JESUS is not inflated, JESUS is not rude, JESUS does not seek JESUS' own interests,

JESUS is not quick-tempered, JESUS does not brood over injury,

JESUS does not rejoice over wrongdoing but rejoices with the truth.

JESUS bears all things, believes all things, hopes all things, endures all things.

JESUS never fails.

If there are prophecies, they will be brought to nothing; if tongues, they will cease;

if knowledge, it will be brought to nothing.

For we know partially and we prophesy partially,

but when the perfect comes, the partial will pass away.

When I was a child, I used to talk as a child, think as a child, reason as a child;

when I became a man, I put aside childish things.

At present we see indistinctly, as in a mirror, but then face to face.

At present I know partially; then I shall know fully, as I am fully known.

So these three remain, faith, hope, and JESUS, but the greatest of these is JESUS.

Replacing the word *love* with JESUS is even more powerful. Great truth radiates from these verses.

Taking it one step further, consider this verse....

My old self has been crucified with Christ. It is no longer I who live, but Christ lives in me. So I live in this earthly body by trusting in the Son of God, who loved me and gave himself for me.
~ Galatians 2:20 (NLT)

Since Christ lives in us, we are empowered to live out those same virtues Jesus models for us. I encourage you to ponder these truths.

> Time seeking Jesus breeds more love in us and our lives.
> Only because Jesus lives in us, are we enabled to love as He does.

May I encourage you to love extravagantly like Jesus.
> Show love.
> Show Jesus.

Remember the great love God has for you. He sent His one and only Son to earth to die for you – what wondrous, magnificent love.

> *Therefore, I, a prisoner for serving the Lord, beg you to lead a*
> *life worthy of your calling, for you have been called by God.*
> *Always be humble and gentle. Be patient with each other, making*
> *allowance for each other's faults because of your love.*
> *~ Ephesians 4:1-2 (NLT)*

28

A Deck of Cards

A deck of cards can remind us of the Bible and even help us pray. Let's explore something important biblically about each of the card numbers. I will only give one relationship for each number, though it is interesting to think of more.

#2   The Bible consists of 2 sections: The Old and New Testament.

#3   The Trinity – 3 in one – God, the Father, Jesus, the Son, and the Holy Spirit.

#4   The New Testament has 4 Gospels—Matthew, Mark, Luke and John.

#5   Jesus turned 5 loaves of bread and 2 fish into enough food for over 5,000 people with 12 basketfuls left over (John 6:9).

#6   In the beginning, God created man in His image on day 6 (Genesis 1:27).

#7   There are 7 colors in the rainbow (Genesis 9).

#8   When Jesus gave the Sermon on the Mount, He proclaimed the 8 Beatitudes (Matthew 5:3-10).

#9   There are 9 fruits of the Spirit (Galatians 5:22).

#10   God presented Moses with 10 Commandments (Exodus 20:2-17).

And…for the grand finale:

J   The Jack, representative of Jesus, the One who died for our sins.

Q   The Queen, representative of Mary, the mother of Jesus.

K   The King, representative of God, our Father, who reigns over everything.

A   I saved this one for last to stress its all-encompassing importance. Consider how it can sometimes be played as a 1, the lowest number, or it can be used as an ace, the highest number. I think it quite fitting that the symbolism of the ace is this. There is only one way to heaven–through Jesus Christ, God's only Son. Yes, God is the beginning and the end–The Alpha and the Omega.

Some other interesting things about a deck of cards:

13 cards in each suit–corresponding to 13 weeks in a quarter of a year.

4 suits–corresponding with the four seasons–winter, spring, summer and fall.

52 cards–corresponding to 52 weeks in a year.

Isn't it great to see how everything in life is truly connected to God, the Creator of the universe, and everything in it? It is a matter of perspective and how we view even the little details in life. His presence is everywhere and in everything.

The next time you play a card game, may you be reminded of the simple parallels a deck of cards has to help you recall God's goodness in all creation. May you even be reminded to slip in a prayer or two thanking God for all He has done.

I am the Alpha and the Omega, the First and
the Last, the Beginning and the End.
~ Revelation 22:13

29

The Loving Father

One of the most well-known Bible stories is found in Luke 15:11-31, "The Parable of the Lost Son" or "The Prodigal Son." A better title for the story might be "The Loving Father."

When I hear this parable, my attention is drawn to the prodigal son, but come along as we delve deeper into all three people in the parable. We will look at the facts and then reflect on lessons we can learn from each person.

A LOOK AT THE FACTS

Facts: Younger Son.

He wanted out of his father's house and life.

He asked for his portion of his father's inheritance, which basically meant he wished his father was dead.

The younger son took his inheritance and lived a wild, carefree life in a distant country.

He squandered his inheritance quickly and was left with nothing. When famine hit the country he was in, he resorted to feeding pigs.

He was starving, so he decided to return to his father's house to work as a hired servant.

He admitted to his father the error of his ways, recognizing he was not worthy to be called, "son."

Facts: Older Son.

He had labored for his father many years.

He was faithful to his father's work.

He obeyed his father's orders.

Facts: The Father.

He gave the younger son his inheritance when asked, though usually it was awarded after death.

He welcomed the estranged younger son home; no questions asked.

His heart was full of compassion for both sons.

He threw a celebration for the younger son when he returned. He put a ring on his finger, sandals on his feet, and killed the fattened calf to celebrate.

He let the older son know he appreciated his faithfulness.

LESSONS FOR REFLECTION

Lessons: The Younger Son.

When he was in a place of total despair and hopelessness, he turned to his father.

Upon returning home, he admitted the error of his ways to the point of feeling unworthy of being called, "son."

He was willing to reap the consequences of his actions.

His heart was transformed and softened. He changed his ways.

Lessons: The Older Son.

He was angry and bitter toward both the father and his younger brother.

He felt he deserved only the finest because he obeyed and slaved for his father.

He was condemning of his younger brother and did not want anything to do with him.

He was more focused on the Law than a heart of love. His heart was hard.

Lessons: The Father.

> He was *generous* in giving the younger son his inheritance as well as sharing all he had with the older son.
>
> He let the younger son *find his own way.* He did not try to force him to stay.
>
> He *welcomed* his estranged son home as soon as he spotted him from a distance.
>
> He had great *compassion* and *love,* wanting the best for both sons.
>
> He knew it was important to *celebrate* his son coming to his senses, from death to life.
>
> He *forgave* the younger son. The past did not matter. He was ready to celebrate and move forward.

What a powerful story; the father in the parable mirrors many of the attributes of God, our Father. Do you view our Heavenly Father as generous, letting you find your own way to Him, always welcoming you with great compassion and love? He is always ready to forgive you and celebrate you. That is exactly why He sent Jesus, His only begotten Son to earth to die for you, so you might be His son or daughter.

Which son do you relate to more—the younger or the older? May your heart remain softened and open to the Father who loves and cares for you.

The Lord is gracious and compassionate; slow to anger and rich in love.
The Lord is good to all; he has compassion on all he has made.
~ Psalm 145:8-9

Christine M. Fisher

30

The Greatest Servant

I know a man who walked this earth a long time ago. His entire life was spent serving everyone. He continually served humankind by physically healing the sick, the lame, and the blind—as well as restoring their souls and spirits. This servant came for everyone. He did not discriminate. In His eyes, no matter how "good" or "bad," all were equal. His love for each person was unconditional in every way.

His servanthood shone forth even on the night he was betrayed by a friend. He "lowered" himself and washed the feet of His friend with love and compassion. The greatest way He served humankind was when He was hanging on a cross. This servant bore our sins and infirmities—He endured the suffering, agony, and pain in order to give us eternal life.

This man's life is a perfect guide for living the life of a true servant. May we serve one another in humility and love as we follow the example of the greatest servant—Jesus Christ.

...Instead, whoever wants to become great among you must be your servant,
and whoever wants to be first must be your slave—just
as the Son of Man did not come to be served,
but to serve, and to give his life as a ransom for many.
~ Matthew 20:26-28

31

Take Care of Them

*If you claim to be religious but don't control
your tongue, you are fooling yourself,
and your religion is worthless. Pure and genuine
religion in the sight of God the Father
means caring for orphans and widows in their distress
and refusing to let the world corrupt you.*
~ James 1:26-27 (NLT)

These Bible verses, when using the terms " religious" and " religion," are referring to the outward acts of being a believer, having a personal relationship with the Lord, doing our acts from the heart. It is not referring to what denomination we are part of. If we are doing acts of service, such as giving to the needy, fasting, or helping others because of our relationship with the Lord, we need to also be watching what comes out of our mouth. If our mouth does not match our actions, our motives are not necessarily pure, which renders our works useless for furthering the kingdom.

God expects us to have a tender heart for the orphans and widows, who in Jesus' day were often neglected rather than cared for. If we do, we are pure and genuine. It is also important that we not let others, who are rebelling or alienated from God, get in the way of our relationship with God and serving others with a pure heart.

The good man brings good things out of the good stored up in his heart, and the evil man brings evil things out of the evil stored in his heart. For out of the overflow of his heart his mouth speaks.
~ Luke 6:45

Christine M. Fisher

How does scripture say we are to live in relation to our hearts, orphans and widows?

For our hearts, we can...

> be in a right relationship with God.
> align our hearts with God.
> guard our tongue and the words we speak.
> encourage and edify others rather than criticize.

Unto orphans, we can ask...

> Is God calling me to bring an orphan into my life to care for?
> If someone I know has foster children, can I lend them a hand?
> Do I know of a child who might need extra prayer, someone who might fall under the category of an orphan?

For widows, we can consider...

> Are there widows in my church I could visit or reach out to?
> Do I know a widow who would be blessed by some talent I have?
> Could I provide a ride to church to an elderly widow who might not otherwise be able to go?

God is calling us to not only reach out to the orphan or widow in the traditional sense of the word but also to anyone we see who needs something. We can do this by...

> sharing our experience of an illness with someone going through the same thing.
> praying for somebody going through a difficult time or needing direction with decision-making.
> letting people know we are praying for them.
> paying for someone's Christian camp experience because they do not have the money to do so.
> offering to hold a foster baby when they are in our path.

adopting a child or being a foster parent. Caring for these little ones also reminds us how we are God's adopted children.

visiting someone in a nursing home.

sponsoring a child or elderly person in a foreign country.

Take time to reflect. Who are the widows and orphans in your life, not just literally but figuratively? Who and what can you do to help take care of them in Jesus' name?

The Spirit of the Lord God is upon me, because the Lord has
anointed me to bring good news to the poor; he has sent me to bind
up the brokenhearted, to proclaim liberty to the captives,
and the opening of the prison to those who are bound;
to proclaim the year of the Lord's favor,
and the day of vengeance of our God; to comfort all who mourn.
~ Isaiah 61:1-2 (ESV)

Christine M. Fisher

32

Beloved

The word *beloved* represents *agapétos* or *agape love* which, in Greek, equates to what we consider a sacrificial love—the highest form of love. What are scriptures passages that reference the word *beloved*? One of the first New Testament references is when John the Baptist baptized Jesus in the Jordan River.

And when Jesus was baptized, immediately he went up from the water, and behold, the heavens were opened to him, and he saw the Spirit of God descending like a dove and coming to rest on him; and behold, a voice from heaven said, "This is my beloved Son, with whom I am well pleased."
~ Matthew 3:16-17 (ESV)

God's voice from heaven announced Jesus as His beloved Son. Yes, Jesus is God's dearly loved Son and is pleased with Him. In fact, rather than call Jesus by name, God calls Him beloved.

The setting of this next verse is when Jesus took Peter, James, and John, the brother of James, up a high mountain and was transfigured, turned into a state of glory, right before their eyes.

He (Peter) was still speaking when, behold, a bright cloud overshadowed them, and a voice from the cloud said, "This is my beloved Son, with whom I am well pleased; listen to him."
~ Matthew 17:5 (ESV)

Notice the voice from heaven announced the same greeting as when Jesus was baptized, with the addition of "listen to him." It is powerful how God used the same sentence both at Jesus' baptism and when He was transfigured, calling Jesus His beloved Son. Some synonyms for the word *beloved* are precious, cherished, treasured, esteemed, revered. What great love God the Father has for His Son, Jesus. Let these verses about the word *beloved* sink into the depth of your heart and being.

See what kind of love the Father has given to us, that we should
be called children of God; and so we are. The reason why the
world does not know us is that it did not know him.
Beloved, we are God's children now, and what
we will be has not yet appeared;
but we know that when he appears we shall be like
him, because we shall see him as he is.
~ 1 John 3:1-2 (ESV)

In the verse above, the writer, John, calls us *beloved*. We are beloved, because we are God's children too. God not only calls His Son, Jesus, *beloved*, but us as well.

Beloved, let us love one another, for love is from God, and
whoever loves has been born of God and knows God. Anyone
who does not love does not know God, because God is love.
In this is love, not that we have loved God but that he loved us and
sent his Son to be the propitiation for our sins. Beloved, if God so loved
us, we also ought to love one another. No one has ever seen God; if we
love one another, God abides in us and his love is perfected in us.
1 John 4:7-8, 10-12 (ESV)

John, once again calling us *beloved*, also calls us to love. Love is from God and since God loves us so much, we need to have that same love for others.

Put on then, as God's chosen ones, holy and beloved,
compassionate hearts, kindness, humility, meekness, and patience.
~ Colossians 3:12 (ESV)

Notice the reference that we are God's chosen ones, even holy and beloved. Just like Jesus' life on earth reflected compassion, kindness, humility, meekness and patience, so we too are called to live in that way, extending those qualities to all we encounter.

Take time to reflect on what it means to be God's *beloved*, the same name He called Jesus. We get to share in the *agape love* God showed Jesus. You and I are loved that much by God our Father.

You, my friend, are ...
precious,
cherished,
treasured,
esteemed,
revered.

This is how much God loves you. God chose to create you and love you— not because of what you do, but because of who He is. Did you notice the word *beloved* can transform into a reminder to BE-LOVED? Be-loved by God.

...I have loved you with an everlasting love; I
have drawn you with loving-kindness.
~ Jeremiah 31:3

33

Words to Live By

Rejoice in the Lord always. I will say it again: Rejoice.
Let your gentleness be evident to all.
The Lord is near. Do not be anxious for anything, but in everything, by
prayer and petition, with thanksgiving, present your requests to God. And
the peace of God, which transcends all understanding, will guard your
hearts and your minds in Christ Jesus. Finally, brothers, whatever is true,
whatever is noble, whatever is right, whatever is pure, whatever is lovely,
whatever is admirable~ if anything is excellent or praiseworthy~ think about
such things. Whatever you have learned or received or heard from me or
seen in me~ put it into practice. And the God of peace will be with you.
~ Philippians 4:4-9

This scripture, written by the apostle Paul, provides a great example of how we should live moment by moment.

What does Paul tell us we should do no matter how we feel?
> *Rejoice* in the Lord. We need to show great joy or delight in the Lord. Even if we are feeling down, we need to turn our hearts toward rejoicing.

When does Paul say we should rejoice?
> *Always.* What? Not only when something goes our way? Not only when we are happy? No. Always. Even when everything seems to be going wrong; even when we do not feel like it.

Christine M. Fisher

What should radiate from our daily lives?

Gentleness. Synonyms for gentleness are words like kindness, tenderness, softness of action. Our gentleness should be evident to all we encounter.

Paul continues,

Do not be anxious for anything, but in everything, by prayer and petition, with thanksgiving, present your requests to God.
~ Philippians 4:6

A definition of the word anxious is experiencing worry, unease or nervousness. Let's reword the first part of the verse, *"Do not experience worry, unease or nervousness for anything."*

What did Paul say we should be anxious about?

Nothing. How would it be to live day by day not being anxious about anything? This is something we need to keep striving for.

What does Paul tell us to do instead of putting our energy into being anxious?

Present our requests to God.

How do we present our requests to God?

Praying and petitioning. With this, we should be showering Him with thanksgiving.

How often should we do this?

All the time, in everything we do. Think about these two statements...

Anxiety and prayer are two great opposing forces. Praying chases anxiety away.

The antidote to worry is thanksgiving, along with prayer and petition. If we are busy being thankful, there is no time to worry.

And the peace of God, which transcends all understanding,
will guard your hearts and your minds in Christ Jesus.
~ Philippians 4:7

What does Paul say is the biggest benefit and gift of living the above way?
God's *peace,* which is the inner tranquility we have knowing God reigns over everything, all the time. Isn't God's peace the most amazing peace?

Is it easy to understand God's peace?
No. God's peace surpasses all understanding. We cannot wrap our human mind around this. It is something we experience.

What will God's peace guard in our lives?
God's peace guards *our hearts and minds* in Jesus. His peace will guide all we do, say and think. What peace we have when we give our concerns to the Lord. This is a powerful way to live.

Finally, brothers, whatever is true, whatever is noble, whatever is
right, whatever is pure, whatever is lovely, whatever is admirable~
if anything is excellent or praiseworthy~ think about such things.
~ Philippians 4:8

What should we be thinking most about in our lives as we live moment by moment?
Whatever is true, noble, right, pure, lovely, and admirable. Anything that is excellent or praiseworthy. Paul knew the influence of one's thoughts and the importance of dwelling on heavenly things. What we allow to occupy our mind will sooner or later come out in speech and action.

Christine M. Fisher

Whatever you have learned or received or heard from me, or seen in me,
put it into practice. And the God of peace will be with you.
~ Philippians 4:9

What does Paul say to do with the things he has shared?

Put them into *practice*. We must not only think on the things in life that are true, noble, right, pure, lovely, admirable, excellent and praiseworthy, but put them into practice following the example Paul lived out. Living this way will result in a life of moral and spiritual excellence, something we can all do.

Try living out one verse for a few days and then progress to the next.

Worry and anxiety can consume our lives preventing us from seeing the love which surrounds us and binds us to one another. Don't miss the forest for the trees. I saw this quote that fits perfectly with these thoughts:

"We are living today what we worried about yesterday." ~ Dale Carnegie

Peace I leave with you; my peace I give you. I
do not give to you as the world gives.
Do not let your hearts be troubled and do not be afraid.
~ John 14:27

34

Jesus' Prayer

"Simon, Simon, Satan has asked to sift you as wheat. But I
have prayed for you Simon that your faith may not fail. And
when you have turned back, strengthen your brothers."
~ Luke 22:31-32

The Lord opened my eyes to see something I had not noticed before. It is a simple thing, but it made me stop and reflect on the specialness of it. It is worth pondering to see what each sentence in the above scripture is saying.

"Simon, Simon, Satan has asked to sift you, as wheat."

Isn't it interesting to note Satan wants to get his hand in everyone's life to try to confuse and make us lose our focus? Just as Satan tried to win control over Jesus' life by tempting Him in the desert, he also tries to rule in our lives.

"But I have prayed for you, Simon that your faith may not fail."

This sentence resonated with me. Jesus prayed for Simon personally, that Simon's faith *not* fail him. Jesus prayed for Simon, that his faith would be bigger in Simon's life than Satan's influence. In more "human" terms, one could argue that God did *not* answer Jesus' prayer, because Simon denied Jesus three times before the cock crowed, just as Jesus had predicted. But we need to look at what else Jesus said.

"But what about you?" he asked. "Who do you say I am?" Simon
Peter answered, "You are the Christ, the Son of the living God."
Jesus replied, "Blessed are you, Simon son of Jonah, for this
was not revealed to you by man, but by my Father in Heaven.

And I tell you that you are Peter, and on this rock I will build
my church, and the gates of Hades will not overcome it."
~ Matthew 16:15-18

...built on the foundation of the apostles and prophets,
with Christ Jesus himself as the chief cornerstone.
~ Ephesians 2:20

With Jesus as the chief cornerstone, Peter (earlier referred to as Simon) is included in the line of apostles and prophets despite originally denying Christ. In his heart, he truly believed Jesus was the Son of God. So, ultimately God answered Jesus' prayer for Simon's faith. It just was not as immediate or timely as we might have expected. I believe Jesus knew Simon would deny Him, yet He still prayed for Simon, especially because of the next verse.

"And when you have turned back, strengthen your brothers."

Jesus knew when Peter's faith returned, it would ultimately strengthen others.

The original Luke passage points out important lessons about prayer that can apply to our lives.

How many times does God not answer our prayer in the way we think He should?
How many times does God not answer our prayer in the timeframe we had in mind?
Everything happens in God's time, under His control, serving His purposes for the best.

And I will do whatever you ask in my name, so that
the Son may bring glory to the Father.
~ John 14:13

35

The Difference

Hearing a talk on a familiar Bible story gave me a different interpretation that I found enlightening; a great truth we can all reflect on and incorporate into our lives. The gospel story is about Martha and Mary (Luke 10:38-42).

Martha was busy serving, which is an important task. If she was not serving, the people might not have had food to eat. Notice how Martha was "distracted" with this serving. What else did Jesus specifically mention to Martha? That she was anxious and troubled by many things. She had not yet come to the point in her life where her relationship with Jesus was most important. She did not have the inner peace that comes from trusting Him.

What did Mary choose to do when Jesus came to their house? She sat at the Lord's feet listening intently to His teaching. Mary wanted to learn more and was interested in what Jesus had to share. Why did Mary choose to focus on listening to Jesus? A valid explanation could be Mary had a personal relationship with Jesus and knew of His importance in her life. She knew in her heart that He was the Messiah; her priorities were straight. Wanting to grow into a deeper relationship with Him drove her to sit at His feet, simply "being" in His presence.

What important by-product of a personal relationship with Jesus did Mary exhibit? Peace. A peace of mind and a peace of heart; a peace that was greater than the circumstances of this life. Mary was content and not anxious as she willingly listened to Jesus; she found what Jesus came to give—true peace in Him.

No Jesus, no peace. Know Jesus, know peace.

Christine M. Fisher

Take a few moments to reflect on your life. Viewing the story of Martha and Mary in this way, are you more like Martha or Mary? We all need a balance of both. If you believe you are more of a Martha, I encourage you to surrender and work on sitting at the feet of Jesus, spending time alone with Him in prayer, reading the Bible, and just being. The more you do it, the closer He will be in your life.

If you believe you are more of a Mary, continue in that deep abiding relationship daily. Be set apart from this world; live differently because of your personal relationship with Jesus. He makes the difference. Live each day, each moment, as Jesus said Mary did.

> *But one thing is necessary; Mary has chosen the good*
> *portion; it will not be taken away from her.*
> ~ Luke 10:42 (ESV)

Know peace, know Jesus. Without Jesus, there is no peace.

> *I am leaving you with a gift—peace of mind and heart.*
> *And the peace I give is a gift the world cannot*
> *give. So don't be troubled or afraid.*
> ~ John 14:27 (NLT)

36

Soar

But those who hope in the Lord will renew their strength.
They will soar on wings like eagles.
~ Isaiah 40:31

What a powerful message and image to reflect on. What if we truly took Isaiah 40:31 to heart and emulated these words? How would it change the way we live?

Let's look at some definitions of hope–a feeling of expectation and desire for a certain thing to happen; a feeling of trust. Notice how both definitions use the word *feeling*. We cannot always trust our feelings, as feelings can change from one minute to the next. Our faith and relationship with the Lord should be based on something concrete.

How about if we viewed "hope in the Lord" more as confident expectation, which equates to faith?

But those who have confident expectation in the Lord...

So, hope in the Lord is not only a feeling, but a stronger confident expectation. Why do I think hope = confident expectation = faith?

Now faith is being sure of what we hope for
and certain of what we do not see.
~ Hebrews 11:1

Christine M. Fisher

Against all hope, Abraham in hope believed and
so became the father of many nations,
just as it had been said to him, "So shall your offspring be."
~ Romans 4:18

In both passages above, the "hope" talked about is equal to *faith*. When do we need to have that confident expectation in the Lord?

When the chips are stacked against us.

When our human eyes see no way out.

When we are at our weakest.

Back to Isaiah 40:31, the promise says, *if* we have that confident expectation, He will renew our strength.

Some ways to be renewed in strength are…

having the graces to make it through our crisis or situation.

knowing that, no matter what, God is in control.

receiving power to face the new day, even when nothing seems right.

They will soar on wings like eagles.

Did you know…

the eagle's wingspan ranges from 6 to 8 feet?

the eagle's wings are lightweight in design weighing less than 2 pounds?

the eagle's wings are stronger than the wing of an airplane?

the bald eagle rarely flaps its wings but soars instead, holding its wings almost completely flat?

the eagle's short tail and broad, long wings allow them to soar high above the open plains and water?

Seeing an eagle soar across the sky is a majestic, beautiful, peaceful scene to behold. What a wonderful image and assurance to know, when going through the difficult times in life, if we keep that confident assurance…

the Lord is there to renew our strength,

and we can soar on His wings,

just as He created the eagles to do.

Soaring high above the cares of this world…

not growing weary,

walking and not becoming faint.

"I carried you on eagles' wings and brought you to myself."
~ Exodus 19:4

37

The Power of Threes

There are numerous scripture passages that enumerate the number "three." Many are references from the New Testament and mostly revolve around Jesus' last days on this earth. (Below, I will give a short description and reference so you can read the stories in your quiet time.)

While Jesus was in Mary's womb, she visited her cousin Elizabeth (whose husband was Zechariah) and stayed three months (Luke 1:56).

When Jesus was 12 years old, Mary and Joseph began their journey home from the Feast of Passover in Jerusalem, accidentally leaving Jesus behind, where he spent three days in the temple (Luke 2:41-52).

When Jesus was tested by Satan in the desert, Jesus quoted three Bible verses to counter each of Satan's three attempts to trick Him (Matthew 4:1-11).

Jesus took three of His disciples, Peter, James and John, to the mountain where He was transfigured before their eyes (Matthew 17:1-12).

Jesus prayed in the Garden of Gethsemane, asking God three times, *"If it be possible, may this cup be taken from me"* (Matthew 26:36-46).

Jesus asked Peter three times, *"Do you love me?"* (John 21:15-17).

Peter denied knowing Jesus three times (Luke 22:54-62).

When Jesus died, He and two robbers were crucified (Matthew 27:38).

There were three hours of darkness while Jesus suffered on the cross (Mark 15:33).

Jesus was crucified at the third hour (Mark 15:25).

After Jesus died, He rose from the dead three days later (Luke 24:8).

After Jesus rose, there were three separate days He appeared to the disciples:

On the road to Emmaus where two disciples were walking, and the same evening to all the disciples except Thomas (Luke 24:13-44). A week later, Jesus appeared to Thomas. By seeing, Thomas believed (Luke 20:24-29).

Jesus appeared to the disciples at the Sea of Tiberias where he provided them with a miraculous catch of fish (John 21:1-14).

Isn't it interesting how the "three" theme starts with God's three main attributes?

God is omnipotent, all powerful.

For by him all things were created, in heaven and on earth, visible and invisible, whether thrones or dominions or rulers or authorities—all things were created through him and for him.
~ Colossians 1:16 (ESV)

God is omniscient, all knowing.

You know what I am going to say even before I say it, Lord.
~ Psalm 139:4 (NLT)

God is omnipresent, all-present.

I can never escape from your Spirit. I can never get away from your presence. If I go up to heaven, you are there; if I go down to the grave, you are there. If I ride the wings of the morning, if I dwell by the farthest oceans, even there your hand will guide me, and your strength will support me.
~ Psalm 139:7-10 (NLT)

Yes, only all-powerful God could be all three things at once. Perhaps all these "three's" serve as a reminder of the most important "three" in our lives…the Trinity—really three separate persons yet one.

> God, the Father,
> Jesus, the Son,
> The Holy Spirit.

Who have been chosen according to the foreknowledge of God the Father, through the sanctifying work of the Spirit, to be obedient to Jesus Christ and sprinkled with his blood: Grace and peace be yours in abundance.
~ 1 Peter 1:2

You are made in God's image; therefore, the Trinity resides within you. Isn't that powerful?

God continued the "three" theme even further by creating within us…
> a body, representing God;
> a soul, representing Jesus;
> and a spirit, representing the Holy Spirit;
> serving as a constant reminder of the Trinity that dwells within us.

> *Now may the God of peace himself sanctify you*
> *completely and may your whole*
> *spirit and soul and body be kept blameless at*
> *the coming of our Lord Jesus Christ.*
> ~ 1 Thessalonians 5:23 (ESV)

One last "three" to serve as a reminder.

> *Three things will last forever—faith, hope, and*
> *love—and the greatest of these is love.*
> ~ 1 Corinthians 13:13 (NLT)

Go, in His name, to love those whose lives you touch. His love for us is truly the greatest.

Christine M. Fisher

38

True Identity

Isn't it easy to fall into the trap of thinking our identity or worth is based on how we "perform?" Isn't it also easy to believe the lies we hear echo in our head?

Have you ever felt your identity is tied to…

your career or job?

what others think of you?

the education/degrees you have?

the things you contribute to make the world a better place?

your physical limitations?

your daily activities?

Do any of these lies sound familiar?

You are not good enough.

You will never be successful.

You are not lovable.

You are not worthy.

You are not beautiful.

I challenge you to think about where your true identity is found. Will you continue to believe the lies? What if…

you were not able to work?

your friends did not talk to you?

you never got that PhD?

you were unable to contribute to this world in the usual ways?

Who would you be then?

Would your world still have purpose?

What if you stopped believing the lies and started believing what God says about you?

Let us explore who we really are, where our identity and worth are found.

Who are we?
WE ARE CHILDREN OF GOD
How great is the love the Father has lavished on us,
that we should be called children of God. And that is what we are.
~ 1 John 3:1

In whose image are we made?
WE ARE CREATED IN GOD'S IMAGE
So God created man in his own image, in the image of God he created him;
male and female he created them.
~ Genesis 1:27

Why are we here?
WE ARE HERE TO GLORIFY GOD
So whether you eat or drink or whatever you
do, do it all for the glory of God.
~ 1 Corinthians 10:31

What is our ultimate goal in life?
OUR ULTIMATE GOAL IS TO SPEND
ETERNITY WITH GOD
For God so loved the world that he gave his one and only Son,
that whoever believes in him shall not perish but have eternal life.
~ John 3:16

How can we overcome the lies we believe?
With the word of God.

I AM GOOD ENOUGH

*But you are a chosen race, a royal priesthood, a holy nation, a people
for his own possession, that you may proclaim the excellencies of
him who called you out of darkness into his marvelous light.*
~ 1 Peter 2:9 (ESV)

I AM SUCCESSFUL

*The Lord will give grace and glory; no good thing will
he withhold from those who walk uprightly.*
~ Psalm 84:11 (NASB)

I AM LOVEABLE

Greater love has no one than this; that he lay down his life for his friends.
~ John 15:13

I AM WORTHY

*Are not two sparrows sold for a penny? Yet not one
of them will fall to the ground apart
from the will of the Father. And even the very
hairs of your head are all numbered.
So don't be afraid; you are worth more than many sparrows.*
~ Matthew 10:29-31

I AM BEAUTIFUL

*Your beauty should not come from outward
adornment, such as elaborate hairstyles
and the wearing of gold jewelry or fine clothes.
Rather, it should be that of your inner self,
the unfading beauty of a gentle and quiet spirit,
which is of great worth in God's sight.*
~ 1 Peter 3:3-4

Try dwelling on your true identity which is found in God and Christ alone. Believe the truths the word of God proclaims of who you really are.

You will keep in perfect peace those whose minds
are steadfast, because they trust in you.
~ Isaiah 26:3

39

Abandonment

Who has abandoned you…whether intentional or not? What situations have made you feel abandoned?

> A parent or spouse who left you?
> A loved one who died unexpectedly?
> A friend who no longer talks to you?
> A significant other you thought you would marry?
> Learning you have an incurable disease?
> Dealing with abuse in your life, whether physical, emotional or sexual?

Often the pain can be devastating. It can take a lifetime to recover. Abandonment can cause grief. The best thing we can do is accept the grief, take time to feel it, and try each day to put one foot in front of the other. We need to hold on to God's promises, the truth, in our feelings of abandonment.

Knowing we are not alone can offer solace for our aching hearts. Jesus experienced feelings of abandonment as He was hanging on the cross.

> *At noon, darkness fell across the land. At about three*
> *o'clock, Jesus called out with a loud voice,*
> *"Eli, Eli, lema sabachthani?" which means "My God,*
> *my God, why have you abandoned me?"*
> ~ Matthew 27:45-46 (NLT)

This was the only time Jesus did not call God "Father," because Jesus took upon Himself *all* the sins of the world—our sins—so we do not have to live under their weight.

Jesus did not sin.

> *He (Christ) committed no sin, neither was deceit found in his mouth.*
> ~ 1 Peter 2:22 (ESV)

We know God is holy; the *only* one who is holy from the beginning of creation.

> *No one is holy like the Lord. There is no one besides*
> *you; there is no Rock like our God.*
> ~ 1 Samuel 2:2 (NLT)

Notice in the following verse, the word "holy" is used three times to describe God. Not only is God holy, but He is holy, holy, holy. It is the only attribute of God that is mentioned three times sequentially in the Bible.

> *And they were calling to one another: "Holy, holy, holy is the Lord Almighty;*
> *the whole earth is full of his glory."*
> ~ Isaiah 6:3

Since God is holy, He is separated from sin; God and Jesus have no sin. When Jesus was on the cross, bearing the weight of all our sins, Jesus was spiritually separated from God for that moment. That is why Jesus felt abandoned by God as He hung on the cross. I imagine the spiritual separation was even more agony than the physical pain Jesus experienced.

> *For God made Christ, who never sinned, to be the offering for our sin,*
> *so that we could be made right with God through Christ.*
> ~ 2 Corinthians 5:21 (NLT)

When you feel abandoned by people, take heart in knowing there is one, and only one, who will never abandon you. God, in His infinite goodness will never abandon you. Here are a few of His promises:

No one will be able to stand against you as long as you live.
For I will be with you as I was with Moses. I
will not fail you or abandon you.
~ Joshua 1:5 (NLT)

Do not be afraid or discouraged, for the Lord will personally go ahead of you.
He will be with you; he will neither fail you nor abandon you.
~ Deuteronomy 31:8 (NLT)

What about the flip side of the abandonment question? Have you ever abandoned God? Sometimes the choices we make create a distance in our relationship with our Heavenly Father.

Maybe we choose…
> a lifestyle of sin, though we know better.
> to stop reading our Bible.
> to stop praying to God.
> not to fellowship with other Christians.
> to have other gods, like money or work.

Why do we abandon God?
> We think we know what is best rather than trusting God.
> We base our actions on the way we feel rather than the truth of God's word.
> We find it easier to follow the ways of the world than walking in God's ways.
> We are selfish and impatient.

Remember, even when we abandon God, He remains faithful and true, always waiting for us to return.

For the word of the Lord is right and true; he is faithful in all he does.
~ Psalm 33:4

40

Praying Like Jesus

I find it fascinating to know those whom Jesus prayed for while He walked this earth. Read John 17:1-26 and reflect on the beauty of this treasured thought.

Jesus prayed for Himself.
> *And now, Father, glorify me in your presence with the glory I had*
> *with you before the world began.*
> *~ John 17:5*

He prayed for His original disciples.
> *I pray for them. I am not praying for the world,*
> *but for those you have given me,*
> *for they are yours.*
> *~ John 17:9*

Jesus prayed for *all* believers and continues to do so.
> *My prayer is not for them (His disciples) alone. I pray also for those who will*
> *believe in me through their message, (all future believers…us) that*
> *all of them may be one, Father, just as you are in me and I am in you.*
> *~ John 17:20-21*

> *Who is to condemn? Christ Jesus is the one who died—*
> *more than that, who was raised—who is at the right*
> *hand of God, who indeed is interceding for us.*
> *~Romans 8:34 (ESV)*

How encouraging to know Jesus personally prays for us. Jesus' prayer was that we might be <u>one</u> with God just as Jesus is one with the Father. May the specialness of knowing Jesus prays for us to be <u>one</u> with God and Jesus bring us peace, comfort, and joy.

I have given them the glory that you gave me, that they may
be <u>one</u> as <u>we</u> are <u>one</u>: I in them and you in me. May they be
brought to complete unity to let the world know that you sent
me and have loved them even as you have loved me.
~ John 17:22-23

Jesus left us a great model of prayer for our lives, relevant even 2,000 years later...

to pray for ourselves.

to pray for our friends and family.

to pray for the unity of the church worldwide to be one with God.

Devote yourselves to prayer, being watchful and thankful.
And pray for us, too, that God may open a door
for our message, so that we may
proclaim the mystery of Christ, for which I am in chains.
Pray that I may proclaim it clearly, as I should.
~ Colossians 4:2-4

41

The Greatest Commandments

"Teacher, which is the great commandment in the Law?" And he said to
him, "You shall love the Lord your God with all your heart and with all
your soul and with all your mind. This is the great and first commandment.
And a second is like it: You shall love your neighbor as yourself."
~ Matthew 22:36-39 (ESV)

Jesus came to show us how to love and how to live out these two greatest
commandments, loving the Lord our God will all our heart, soul, and
mind, and loving others as our self.

Didn't Jesus...

> continually pray to God, often taking quiet time away to converse
> with God?
> continually seek God's will, even surrendering to God's plan of
> dying on the cross to set us free?
> even at the young age of 12, show how much He loved God when
> He was left in the Temple, seeking to learn more of God?

Think about the people Jesus associated with and loved. Jesus loved the
outcasts, the marginalized, and the sinners. Jesus loved everyone. From the
woman caught in adultery, to the leper, to the rich man who did not want
to give up his possessions, to Judas, His betrayer. Yes, Jesus even loved His
betrayer. Jesus included him as a friend to share in His last supper.

One of Jesus' greatest acts was loving those who put Him to death. Jesus
said,

"Father, forgive them, for they do not know what they are doing."
And they divided up his clothes by casting lots.
~ Luke 23:34

Take a few moments to evaluate how well you live out these two greatest commandments.

> Do you really love the Lord your God with all your heart, soul, and mind?
>
> Do you strive to put God above all else, all other false gods in your life?
>
> Do you continually converse with God throughout the day, not just when you go to church?
>
> Do you take time to listen to God?
>
> Do you take time to be still with God, to dig into His word and see how it applies to your life?
>
> Do your actions show that you love your neighbor—those you know and even strangers?

An acquaintance shared this story that brought a new level of meaning to loving our neighbor. He was going through training to be a hospice volunteer. The thought that he might have to tend to the needs of an incontinent person, perhaps changing and cleaning a person, almost led him to abandon the idea. He wrestled for a while trying to figure out why it bothered him so much.

One day while babysitting his two-year-old grandson, he had to change a diaper. It suddenly hit him what the ministry issue was about. He had such great unconditional love for his grandson that changing a diaper was not bothersome. Could he have that same unconditional love for a stranger who Jesus calls his neighbor? Could he...

> Humble himself?
>
> Be vulnerable enough?

Bring himself to clean and change someone, a stranger, a neighbor who was in need?

He was finally able to say yes. He was willing to truly love a stranger and do anything the person needed physically. He was at peace. Through all his years volunteering, he never had to face that situation.

Do you really *love* your neighbor? Are you willing to humble yourself, being vulnerable, surrendering your pride, and willing to meet whatever needs they have? Does your love know no boundaries, doing whatever it takes to put *love* into action...to live out Jesus' commandment to love others as yourself?

Try to live out the two greatest commandments. Keep stretching yourself, growing in Him, reflecting Him to others, and making disciples of all.

This is my commandment: Love each other in the same way I have loved you.
There is no greater love than to lay down one's life for one's friends.
~ John 15:12-13 (NLT)

Christine M. Fisher

42

Ponder These Things

Below are two phrases from the Bible that spark a chord in my heart.

*But Mary treasured up all these things and
pondered all these things in her heart.*
~ Luke 2:19

His mother treasured all these things in her heart.
~ Luke 2:51

The first verse is shortly after Jesus' birth. An angel of the Lord appeared to the shepherds announcing the birth of Christ. Once the shepherds saw Jesus lying in the manger, they spread the words the angel told them. How amazing to think that Mary, the mother of Jesus, took time and pondered these things in her heart.

The second verse is when Jesus was 12 years old. Mary and Joseph took Jesus to Jerusalem to celebrate the Feast of the Passover. When Mary and Joseph were headed home, a day into the trip, they realized Jesus was missing. Three days later they found him teaching in the temple. Jesus told Mary,

"Didn't you know I had to be in my Father's house?"
~ Luke 2:49

Again, Mary treasured all these things in her heart. I think we can relate with Mary on many levels.

She was willing to do what God asked of her—to be the mother of Jesus rather than saying no.

She pondered in her heart what Jesus' life would be like rather than announcing to everyone He was the Holy One.

She treasured the thoughts of what Jesus would do for His Father rather than getting angry at him for not being with them.

She released Jesus back to God, knowing He was sent to do God's will. Imagine watching your son suffer an excruciating, painful death on a cross.

What hardship Mary endured as the mother of Jesus, yet she left us a wonderful example. If she, being the mother of Jesus, pondered and treasured all these events in her life, how much more should we ponder and treasure the words and parables Jesus shared with us?

Do you ever "ponder" or "treasure" things in your heart? It is probably a natural thing to do, especially if you are a parent. Different milestones in your child's life might be something you ponder or treasure. How about scripture passages or prayers for people? Do you "ponder" or "treasure" those things in your heart? How about the many "God incidents" you experience? Do you share them with others to strengthen their faith?

Mary lived a gentle, humble life pondering and treasuring even the little things. Let us strive to do the same.

Reflect on what I am saying, for the Lord will give you insight into all this.
~ 2 Timothy 2:7

Christine M. Fisher

43

Perfect Love

There is no fear in love, but perfect love casts out fear.
For fear has to do with punishment, and whoever
fears has not been perfected in love.
~ 1 John 4:18 (ESV)

Fear is first mentioned in the Garden of Eden after Adam and Eve ate the fruit from the forbidden tree. What does this tell us about fear? Fear is from Satan, not God. The garden, once a paradise where Adam and Eve enjoyed fellowship with God, suddenly involved the element of fear. Fear, like sin, separates us from God. Adam and Eve feared God would punish them for being naked, so they tried to hide from God (Genesis 3:6-10).

How do we handle fear? Perfect love casts out fear. Consider these lessons from scripture:

Anyone who does not love does not know God, because God is love.
~ 1 John 4:8 (ESV)

So we have come to know and to believe the love that God has for us.
God is love, and whoever abides in love abides
in God, and God abides in him.
~ 1 John 4:16 (ESV)

Who is love and where does it come from? God is love and love comes from God. Since God is equal to love, let's look at 1 John 4:18 and substitute the word *love* with *God*.

There is no fear in GOD, but perfect GOD casts out fear.
For fear has to do with punishment, and whoever
fears has not been perfected in GOD.

How powerful is that? The antidote to fear is faith and trust in God. Consider these passages as examples:

Shadrach, Meshach and Abednego did not let fear or the risk of losing their life prevent them from professing their faith in God. Their faith and trust in God were so great they knew He would protect them. Even if it was not God's will for them to survive the blazing furnace, they would not disobey Him by bowing down to idols. Their love for God was as evident as the faith and trust they had in Him (Daniel 3:16-28).

Mary was asked to embark on a great adventure by being the mother of Jesus, the Savior of the world. One of the first things the angel said to her was, *"Do not be afraid, Mary."* Mary is quite the example of embracing faith and trust rather than fear. With love, she graciously said yes to God's plan (Luke 1:28-31).

Jesus, fully knowing it was time for His death, once more asked God if there was another way for salvation to come to the world. Deep down Jesus knew the cup could not be removed from Him. He did not face the plan with fear, but rather with the love of a son for His Father. Jesus had complete faith and trust in fulfilling God's plan of salvation that is offered to all. What an ultimate sacrifice for you and me (Luke 22:39-44).

Stephen was not afraid to stand up for his faith in God even to the point of death by stoning. His love, faith, and trust in God alone were greater than any other power in his life. How fascinating to see how similar Stephen's story is to what Jesus endured in His final days on earth (Acts 6:11-15, Acts 7:59-60).

There is no fear in love, but perfect love casts out fear.
For fear has to do with punishment, and whoever
fears has not been perfected in love.
~ 1 John 4:18 (ESV)

If you have accepted Christ as your Lord and Savior, asking for your sins to be forgiven, there is no longer any punishment or judgment for your sins awaiting you. Therefore, there is no condemnation, no fear of God's judgment, because God's genuine love is present with salvation. In addition, as a believer continually communing with God, Jesus and the Holy Spirit, we have nothing to fear. God is love and we have the victory in Him. Fear does not rule our lives; fear is from Satan. With God, we can dispel fear as we continually exercise our faith and trust in God alone.

Day by day, one situation at a time, strive to cast out fear. Have faith and trust in God. How? By standing on the promises of God's word which reminds us…

God is always with us.

God works all things out for our good.

God is trustworthy.

God is our strong tower.

our faith and trust in God are bigger than any fear we might have.

For God gave us a spirit not of fear but of power and love and self-control.
~ 2 Timothy 1:7 (ESV)

44

The Potter's Masterpiece

Read Jeremiah 18:1-10 and Isaiah 64:8. The images of the potter and the masterpiece are powerful.

HAVE YOU PICTURED YOURSELF AS THE CLAY AT THE MERCY OF THE POTTER'S HAND?

I have always interpreted these verses as acknowledging God as the Father and humans as the clay, being shaped and molded into the people He desires. What I did not think about was the free will God granted us. Jeremiah 18:4 seems to support that idea:

And whenever the clay would not take the shape he wanted,
he would change his mind and form it into some other shape.

When we watch a potter's wheel, we observe the clay constantly moving and shifting. The potter constantly adds water to the clay, shaping and reshaping. Can't that be representative of our lives because of the free will we have? Is it possible God gave us free will to first see how sincere our hearts are, as well as to show how great a God He really is?

If, in our free will, our hearts are sincere and seek to please God, He won't have to reshape us too much, will He? He shapes and helps us become the best version of ourselves.

If, in our free will, we don't allow Him access to our hearts, minds, and actions, the reshaping we do of our own lives begins to resemble the world rather than the person God created us to become. If we yield and return to Him, our lives can be placed back on the potter's wheel. His gentle and firm hand can begin the process of reshaping us into His likeness. When we allow Him to, God can reshape the clay and work things so we can see how He truly is God of all.

Wouldn't God's work be much simpler if He did not give us the gift of free will? If we were just a piece of marble or clay free-forming on a table, that would be much easier for Him. Thankfully, He did not make us that way. We can be continually reminded of His greatness since He can take our choices and our actions and still form something beautiful from our messes and missteps.

We have the privilege and challenge of honoring God, the Potter, in all we do, with the way, we, the clay, interact with others and the way we love Him. God is not a passive God who sits back and watches our lives unfold. No, He is the Potter always at work helping to shape our lives to make us more like Him, so we can reflect His love to all we encounter.

Here are some ways the Potter shapes our lives daily:
> If we mess up and turn back to Him, He takes our mess and uses it for His good.
> He whispers in our heart which way we should go.
> He nudges us when we need to step out and encourage another.
> He speaks to others to minister to or encourage us when we need it most.
> He gives us faith to do things we never envisioned.

Keep in mind:
> God makes something beautiful out of every piece of clay He forms.
> No matter what we do with our lives, the Potter can reshape us if we turn back to Him.
> The Potter can take our choices and actions, even the bad ones, and form something beautiful, if we yield our lives to Him.

Thank you for making me so wonderfully complex.
Your workmanship is marvelous—how well I know it.
~ Psalm 139:14 (NLT)

45

My Favorite Bible Verse

This has been my favorite Bible verse since my teenage years:

And we know that in all things God works for
the good of those who love him,
who have been called according to his purpose.
~ Romans 8:28

Keep in mind these two conditions for God to *work all for our good:* we are called to love God and to be called according to His purposes.

Loving God is coming to the point in life where we surrender everything to Him. We realize everything we have and everything we are is a gift from Him. Being *called according to His purposes* is knowing He calls us to do His will and then following His will—not ours.

My faith is always strengthened by seeing how God truly works things out. One example is the year my oldest son needed to have his wisdom teeth pulled. We wanted it done during his summer break from college and before our vacation. There was a Monday appointment available that would work perfectly. By the time the doctor saw the x-rays, only 24 hours after the initial phone call, the Monday appointment had been taken. The next available appointment was two weeks later, which did not fit well with our vacation plans. I asked to be put on a cancellation list, unhappy my plan was not working out as I thought it should. I reluctantly turned it over to the Lord, asking Him to work it out.

Much to my amazement, two days later the dentist office called. They had a cancellation for that very afternoon. To make it more amazing, my son had not eaten or drank anything since the night prior, which was a requirement. God worked it out perfectly.

Can you think of examples when God worked things for your good?

It is a comfort and joy to know that God takes care of everything and works it for our good if we love Him and are called according to His purposes. No matter what comes our way, our loving Father is working it all out for our good—He is watching over us. We need to remain faithful to Him and keep loving Him.

The Lord watches over all who love him, but all the wicked he will destroy.
~ Psalm 145:20

46

Lessons for the Storms

I have come to appreciate the Bible story of Jesus walking on the water. Below are key thoughts to ponder from the scripture (Matthew 14:22-34).

> Jesus *made* the disciples get into the boat without Him; this was part of God's plan.
> Jesus went to the mountainside alone to pray.
> Jesus was with His Father for several hours while the disciples were alone in the boat.
> The wind caused big waves which moved the boat about.
> Jesus went to the boat (walking on the water) sometime between 3 a.m. and 6 a.m.
> Peter was brave enough to step out of the boat and start walking to Jesus.
> More people came to believe in Jesus because they realized He was the Son of God.

KEY LESSONS TO KEEP IN MIND DURING THE STORMS IN OUR LIVES

Even the storms in our lives are of divine appointment. Jesus *made* the disciples get in the boat without Him.

Jesus sometimes creates the storms in our lives. When Jesus sent the disciples to the boat, He already knew how it was going to work out; He was in control of the storm.

Even when we cannot see Jesus in the storm we are going through, Jesus sees us. The disciples could not see Him clearly when He was walking on the water because of the storm and the darkness.

The storms of our lives should remind us to stand on the promises of God. When the disciples first saw someone coming toward the boat, Jesus reminded them to not be afraid.

Jesus comes to us in the storms of life at just the right time. He comes at our point of desperation when we are broken to the core.

Jesus walked on the water to help save the disciples from their fear of being overtaken by the wind and water. What we fear might be Jesus in disguise. The wind that brought the storm is the same wind that brought Jesus to them, as He walked on the water.

Jesus is above our storm. The same water that threatened to go *over* the disciples and the boat is the water that was *under* Jesus' feet.

Our ability to walk on water during the storms of life depends on our focus. We are to keep our eyes and heart on Jesus. When Peter stepped out of the boat, he walked on water because his eyes were on Jesus. When he looked at the wind and water, he became afraid and started to sink. When we focus on the obstacles or the storm and take our eyes off Jesus, we sink.

Jesus responds immediately when we cry out in fear. The disciples cried out in fear when they thought a ghost was walking on the water. When Peter began sinking, he cried out to Jesus. Jesus *immediately* responded.

Jesus listens to even the shortest of prayers. Peter only had time to cry out three words, "Lord, save me," in his moment of desperation.

Jesus wants our faith to be greater than our fears or doubt. He said to Peter, "You of little faith, why did you doubt?"

Jesus comes to us in our storms and enters the boat with us. After taking Peter's hand, they both climbed into the boat with the disciples.

When Jesus is in the boat with us, the storm eventually dies down. As soon as Jesus and Peter got in the boat, the wind died down. Yes, Jesus is in control of the wind and the water.

While walking through the storms in life, be reminded…
> Jesus is still sovereign over the storms.
> to trust Jesus even when the wind is blowing, and the waves are crashing around your boat.
> to bring Jesus into your storm.
> to walk on the water with your focus on Jesus.
> Jesus is always working on your behalf.
> Jesus died on the cross with your storm on His mind.

> *O Lord God of hosts, who is mighty as you are,*
> *O Lord, with your faithfulness all around you?*
> *You rule the raging of the sea; when its waves rise, you still them.*
> ~ Psalm 89:8-9 (ESV)

47

Letting Go

Letting go can be a difficult task. What are some common things we might have to let go?

> The security of our familiar surroundings if a job relocates us.
>
> Our good health when suddenly an unexpected crisis occurs.
>
> The proximity of a child who moves halfway across the world.
>
> A relationship that cannot be reconciled.
>
> A person whom we love dearly passes from this life.
>
> When the direction of our life might not line up with God's way.

GOD EXPERIENCED LETTING GO

God let go of His only Son. He sent Jesus to earth to be the atoning sacrifice for our sins. Jesus left paradise and union with God, for a time. How pained God's heart must have been to be physically separated from Jesus while He lived on earth, accomplishing the goal of redemption. Letting go meant seeing Jesus mocked, beaten, and hung on a cross. All so *those who believe* in Jesus can spend eternity with Him.

WHAT ABOUT MARY, THE MOTHER OF JESUS?

Mary, an innocent young woman, was told by an angel that she had been chosen to be the mother of Jesus, the Savior of the world. I am sure she, like any mother, became attached to her son as she watched him grow. Remember the story from Luke 2:41-52 when Jesus was left in the temple? When they found Jesus, He asked, "Didn't you know I had to be in my Father's house?" It appears Mary did not understand exactly what Jesus meant. I have an inkling, shortly after that day, Mary began the letting go process of Jesus, releasing Him bit by bit to God, the Father. Letting go of

Jesus to travel and do His ministry work. Letting go of Jesus as she stood by the cross watching Him give up His life. What agony and heartache she must have felt. How difficult letting go is.

WHAT ABOUT JESUS?

Jesus experienced letting go when He walked this earth. One time was when Jesus, shortly before He was put to death, prayed in the Garden of Gethsemane, "My Father, if it is possible, may this cup be taken from me" (Matthew 26:36-46). His ultimate act of letting go was a spiritual separation from God as He was on the cross, taking the weight of all our sins upon Himself.

> *And about the ninth hour Jesus cried out with a loud*
> *voice, saying, "Eli, Eli, lema sabachthani?"*
> *that is, "My God, my God, why have you forsaken me?"*
> ~ Matthew 27:46 (ESV)

Jesus experienced a letting go of His will; a surrendering to His Father. Jesus and God both experienced letting go, through a spiritual separation, so *we* don't have to. May it bring comfort to know what we are experiencing was even experienced by Jesus and our Heavenly Father.

WE ARE NOT ALONE IN LETTING GO.
OUR FATHER UNDERSTANDS AND IS WITH US.

> *For we do not have a high priest who is unable to*
> *sympathize with our weaknesses, but one who in every*
> *respect has been tempted as we are, yet without sin.*
> ~ Hebrews 4:15 (ESV)

Section 3

GOD'S PRESENCE ILLUMINATED IN PEOPLE

I will praise you, O Lord, with all my heart; I will tell of all your wonders.
~ Psalm 9:1

When Jesus walked this earth, He called people to follow Him. Those people immediately left everything and went with Jesus.

Following Jesus meant learning from Him, listening to Him teach about God, His Father. They were witnesses of the way Jesus lived, loving all He encountered, and healing the sick among them. Jesus' followers could not help but be amazed and in awe of the wonders they saw. Praising Jesus was part of their life.

After Jesus died and rose again, before He ascended back to His Father, He instructed His disciples, "Go, preach the Good News of salvation to the whole world."

God's presence illuminated in people.

48

God in the Ordinary

One day a lady I was talking to repeated something I just said to her, "God in the ordinary." That phrase clicked with her and she said it was like in Jesus' day. The Jews were looking for a king thinking He would come with great fanfare. Instead, God chose to send Jesus, His Son, to this earth as an ordinary man.

**The Jews were not looking for God in the ordinary,
yet that was exactly His plan of redemption.**

How often we are like the Jews from Jesus' day, looking for God to appear with fanfare, thinking He will send a lightning bolt to get our attention. Do we miss seeing God at work in the ordinary? Maybe that is how He wants to get our attention, so we know He is always with us, working in and through us.

Look for God in the ordinary everyday little details in life. Maybe God's presence in the ordinary will be found in…

a hug from your toddler.

an unexpected visit from a friend or family member.

the text saying you are being lifted in prayer.

the gently falling rain.

talking with a person who helped you see something differently.

knowing you helped support a worthy cause.

seeing your child achieve another milestone in life.

Have you recently seen God in the ordinary things of life?

So here's what I want you to do, with God's help. Take your
everyday, ordinary life—your sleeping, eating, going-to-work, and
walking-around life—and place it before God as an offering.

Embracing what God does for you is the best thing you can do for Him.

Don't become so well-adjusted to your culture that
you fit into it without even thinking.
Instead, fix your attention on God.
~ Romans 12:1-2 (MSG)

49

The Mountain Top

One summer I had the pleasure of going to Wind River Ranch in Estes Park, Colorado. This is a Christian family dude ranch located in a wooded area between two mountain ranges. They offer wood cabin lodging, home-cooked meals, spiritual recreation and a variety of activities. This beautiful ranch also afforded me the opportunity of a true mountaintop experience. It granted me a glimpse of heaven on earth, making me feel special, loved, and valued – like royalty!

What was it about Wind River Ranch that provided this mountain top experience?

> God's presence in the beauty of the area.
> The peacefulness of the holy ground surrounding me.
> The way staff interacted with guests, using words and actions to reflect Christ.
> Being with a group of like-minded Christians.
> Having daily devotions and worship.
> The meals prepared and provided by the loving chef and crew.
> The opportunity to focus on my relationship with God.
> An array of activities to stretch me beyond my comfort zone.
> Engaging in meaningful conversations with staff and guests.
> Observing the college-aged young adults volunteering and serving others.
> No worries or obligations for the week.
> Free to just *be* and enjoy the setting and people.
> Being ministered to in body, mind, and soul.

THE WARM WELCOME

When guests arrive at the ranch early enough, two wranglers on horses provide an escort to the top of the property where the Wind River Ranch family greets them. We arrived late, so we did not get the wrangler escort, but our welcome was still warm and sincere. Plates of food were promptly served while staff moved our car to the parking area and delivered our luggage to our cabin.

Do not neglect to show hospitality to strangers, for
thereby some have entertained angels unawares.
~ Hebrews 13:2 (ESV)

ASK AND YOU WILL RECEIVE

Our every need was anticipated and met. Whether we needed a replacement Keurig machine, wood for our fireplace, or cream for our coffee, we just said the word and the items suddenly appeared. *Pampered* is the word to describe how the staff cared for us.

And I tell you, ask, and it will be given to you;
seek, and you will find; knock, and it will be opened to you.
~ Luke 11:9 (ESV)

ENCOURAGE AND PRAY FOR ONE ANOTHER

When the housekeeping staff turned down our beds each night, they placed Bible verses on our pillows, leaving the perfect and uplifting thought we needed to hear. (I hope they were also blessed when we left notes for them.)

While we were walking one day, the college-aged men came alongside some of the older guests, offering to help them climb the steep stairs, or carry items for them. They offered assistance and encouragement.

I witnessed the young adults and staff members, while listening and conversing with guests, offer to pray right at the moment, because they were putting their faith into action. All the staff was willing to pray or talk whenever the need arose.

My last horse trail ride was extra special. My wrangler engaged in meaningful conversation as we were riding and, much to my surprise, she blessed me by sharing her thoughts, which ministered to and encouraged me.

> *Therefore encourage one another and build one*
> *another up, just as you are doing.*
> ~ 1 Thessalonians 5:11 (ESV)

FEEDING THE HUNGRY

The food service at Wind River Ranch was outstanding, providing a variety of buffet food each day. During each meal, we observed how the young adult staff allowed the guests to go through the buffet line first. They would mingle with the guests, striking up conversations wherever they sat. They genuinely cared for everyone and put others before themselves in their interactions. The highlight was Friday evening when we were served a sit-down dinner by the young adults.

> *If you pour yourself out for the hungry and satisfy the desire of the afflicted,*
> *then shall your light rise in the darkness and your gloom be as the noonday.*
> ~ Isaiah 58:10 (ESV)

Reflecting on my time at Wind River Ranch, my royal-mountaintop experience, a foretaste of heaven, I cannot help but think this is exactly how we should live each day.

> *But you are a chosen people, a royal priesthood, a*
> *holy nation, God's special possession,*

that you may declare the praises of him who called
you out of darkness into his wonderful light.
~ 1 Peter 2:9

Yes, *we* are God's chosen, belonging to the *royal* family of God, His *treasured possession.* Every moment of our lives should be spent declaring the *praises* of God. By the sacrifice of His only Son, Jesus, God calls us out of darkness into His wonderful light.

For I was hungry and you gave me food, I was
thirsty and you gave me drink,
I was a stranger and you welcomed me.
~ Matthew 25:35 (ESV)

Christine M. Fisher

50

One Act

While attending a concert of a Christian artist, I saw a short video entitled "One Act" from Compassion International, a child sponsorship program. This caused me to reflect on the truth of how "one act" can make a world of difference in our lives, which was exactly the message the musician was making. He started the segment by sharing his personal testimony. Sixteen years earlier, his life was not in a good place, he had no money, yet he sensed God calling him to a mission trip to the Dominican Republic. Because an acquaintance paid for his plane ticket, that "one act" led him to come to know God in a personal way, which changed the trajectory of his life. It was exactly what he needed to truly surrender to God.

After this concert, I witnessed two "one acts" from the musicians. As the keyboardist was helping tear down the merchandise table, he noticed a young boy and learned it was his birthday. He asked the boy, "Do you want something for your birthday?" The boy nodded and his eyes lit up when he was handed a hat, just like the band member was wearing. I am sure the boy will not soon forget the "one act" he was shown, especially when he wears the hat.

Another musician reached out to a young boy with autism. He talked and joked with the boy, trying to guess his name. The boy's mom was able to get a picture of them despite the fact the boy would not make eye contact and continued to look at the floor. As soon as the picture was taken, the boy looked up and walked out the door. I heard the mother ask the boy if he was happy, and he said, "Yes." I smiled as I watched this tender interaction. What a wonderful "one act" I am sure the boy and his mother will not forget. I bet the boy feels special knowing this musician took time to talk with him, showing he is loved.

Both "one acts" touched my heart. When attending Christian concerts, I am blessed and inspired to see the genuine kindness and character the musicians display. My life is richer because I have had the opportunity to meet and talk with many of these musicians on a personal level. Their acts of kindness remind me what Jesus would do if I met Him.

Try to keep forefront in your mind how "one act" can make a difference in someone's life. What "one act" can you do to bless someone? What will it be?

Helping change a child's life through sponsorship?

Giving someone money to help get medical care?

Singing Christmas carols for a shut-in?

Serving someone a meal?

Adopting a family during the holiday season?

Taking time to listen to someone who is weighed down with burdens?

Praying for someone who is struggling?

Then the King will say, "I'm telling the solemn truth:
Whenever you did one of these things to someone overlooked or ignored,
that was me—you did it to me."
~ Matthew 25:40 (MSG)

51

Celebrate Your Life

When you think about your birthday, what kind of feelings does that elicit? Feelings of happiness or dread? As I have gotten older, I find it easier to think about the negative aspect of birthdays, you know, the aging body having more aches and pains and not working as well as it did. I think it is good to shift our focus to celebrating *us*.

Think about when we hear of someone expecting a child, especially a first time parent. There is so much joy and happiness in celebrating this new life. We think of all the hopes and dreams we have for this child and what the future will be like for him/her.

It seems God wants us to rejoice in those same ways once a year when our birthday rolls around. There are so many things to celebrate. After all, we are God's child…a great reason to celebrate. Over the years, I have grown to appreciate the specialness of my birthday. It reminds me that I am special to the Lord, and He is Lord of *all* creation.

Birthdays make me think about the reasons to celebrate in the Lord…
>the fact my life is a *gift* from God.
>the *miracle* of my life.
>how *special* and *unique* the Lord made me.
>the fact He knew me even while I was in my mother's *womb*.
>the fact He has a divine *purpose* for my life.

Birthdays are also a great time to take inventory of how far we have come in our walk with the Lord and the direction we are heading. So, on your birthday do not worry about getting older, but rather, rejoice and celebrate the fact you are a special part of God's creation.

For you created my inmost being; you knit me together in my mother's womb. I praise you because I am fearfully and wonderfully made; your works are wonderful, I know that full well.
~ Psalm 139:13-14

52

Like-Minded Blessings

Have you noticed and experienced extra blessings when you take time to fellowship with like-minded believers? Each of our stories are so important and worth sharing.

I had the honor of helping my youngest son's preschool teacher in her class. We bonded during our time of working together. Even though she moved two hours away, we have kept in touch. Those times are always special and seem to be when we need like-minded blessings.

One meeting was extra special because it was the first time she insisted on driving to me. We took time to stroll down memory lane to see her old houses and neighborhoods. It was God's perfect timing orchestrated, in that, she was able to see my son, who was then a senior in high school. It was the first time they had seen each other in at least five years.

Another time of receiving a like-minded blessing was attending the concert of a Christian singer, Weston Skaggs. I had never seen him in person, but I followed him on social media and was impressed by his story and faith. After a busy Friday of commitments, I sat down at my computer to check on his upcoming concert in the area. His website said the concert was Saturday, but when I messaged him to confirm, he said he was headed to the venue that very night to perform. It was a God thing that he responded right away.

I quickly grabbed what I needed and arrived 15 minutes after it was slated to start. Much to my surprise, Weston said the concert had been delayed (I think for me). He had just started his first song when I walked in. Time flew by and I did not want the music to stop. At the end of the concert, which was an intimate gathering, the pastor came to talk with me, followed by Weston. It was easy to find common ground in talking with them. I left the church feeling refreshed and my heart was full of peace and joy. Being with like-minded people afforded me many blessings that evening.

I am thankful for the like-minded people I share life with and the opportunities to touch others' lives, all because of Jesus. These people are a source of encouragement and joy. May these thoughts encourage you to take a little time to spend with those like-minded people in your life. Take time to share your story with the people whose lives you touch and even someone you do not personally know. These are the important things. You will be greatly blessed.

For where two or three gather together as my
followers, I am there among them.
~ Matthew 18:20 (NLT)

53

Pearls of Wisdom

"Everything happens for a reason."
"You choose what bothers you."

My son loves to play baseball saying, "Baseball is life." Two years in a row, he was injured and sidelined for the season. The next fall and winter, he worked out three times a week at a gym with a trainer, doing intense workouts to help him gain more strength and muscle. He started eating healthier, drinking only water and incorporating specific physical therapy exercises into his routine. Any moment he was free, he was at our local indoor baseball facility practicing; taking ground balls, hitting, and soaking up whatever a coach advised him to do.

School tryouts for the varsity baseball team were held and the boys learned their fate at the end of practice on the last day. I was attending a meeting that day, so I asked him to let me know as soon as he found out. "Didn't make it," showed up on my phone in the middle of the meeting. My heart sank. I felt bad for him, knowing how hard he had worked, his love for baseball, and how he counted it an honor to play for the school team.

I texted back, "I am so sorry. My heart is breaking for you." I wished I was there to give him a hug to maybe help ease the pain. At that point, I basically tuned out of the meeting, lost in thoughts of my son. "Just no spot for me. He (the coach) told me I am a good ballplayer." We exchanged a few more sentences before I received one saying, *"Everything happens for a reason."* This brought me first to tears, then back to my senses, thinking what an admirable way to look at the situation. The end of his text said, "It happened. It's fine. I'm really not that upset."

Instead of feeling sorry for himself, my son was looking for the positive, making the best of a defeat. I told him not making the team was harder on me than him. It is natural, as parents, to want the best for our children and want their hopes and dreams to come true. Isn't it better, instead of dwelling on the negativity, to think that yes, everything happens for a reason, and it really is fine? Yes, my son set my thinking right that night. His outlook reminded me of the saying, "When life hands you lemons, make lemonade."

"You choose what bothers you." My son mentioned how some people do not think this statement rings true. In the case of my son not making the school team, he could have been angry and upset, letting it bother him and affect his outlook on life, but who is that helping? No one. Would it change the original outcome? No. Would being angry and upset solve anything other than making him miserable? No. By choosing to not let the final result of not making the school baseball team bother him, my son chose to let it go. He surrendered to the fact that it happened, and moved on to what he could do—like continuing to go to the indoor facility to practice and play baseball.

May you be reminded that no matter what you are walking through or experiencing, everything happens for a reason, and you choose what bothers you. Make a conscious decision to look for the positive and the things you can do to live in peace.

How perfect that I heard this today: "Disappointments just might be God's way of saying, 'I've got something better for you, my child.'"

> *The Lord Almighty has sworn, "Surely, as I have planned, so it will be, and as I have purposed, so it will stand."*
> ~ Isaiah 14:24

Christine M. Fisher

54

Just Be Held

Where your passion meets your compassion, there is your gift.

One of my passions is to hold babies and love on them. There is something so sweet and precious about snuggling with this loving, innocent creation that God formed. All life, especially human life, is a sacred and magnificent miracle from God.

> *You made all the delicate, inner parts of my body*
> *and knit me together in my mother's womb.*
> *Thank you for making me so wonderfully complex!*
> *Your workmanship is marvelous*
> *– how well I know it.*
> ~ Psalm 139:13-14 (NLT)

Holding babies in the NICU at a local hospital is a favorite ministry. As I was scrubbing up one day, I could hear a little one crying. He was the one the nurses let me hold first. As soon as I scooped this fellow up, he became calmer and did not cry during the two hours I held and loved him. He did squirm a tad and spit up a little more, but then he seemed content. When I first held him, I embraced him with both arms so he felt safe as I stood swaying with him for a while, before finally settling into the rocking chair.

The words "just be held" popped into my head. It made me think of how often we need to just be held by the Lord...

knowing we are safe in His arms.

knowing everything will be okay.

to soothe our restless hearts.

to calm our fears.

His arms are always ready to embrace us.

So he returned home to his father. And while he was still a
long way off, his father saw him coming. Filled with love and
compassion, he ran to his son, embraced him, and kissed him.
~ Luke 15:20 (NLT)

My arms get tired from holding a baby in the same position for a long period of time, so I found myself changing arms and positions with this little guy. My favorite way to hold a baby is snuggling them against my chest to feel their heartbeat and gentle breathing even more. As I snuggled this baby, I found myself breathing life over him. It reminded me of God breathing life into each of us, His spirit covering us with His love and protection.

For the Spirit of God has made me, and the
breath of the Almighty gives me life.
~ Job 33:4 (NLT)

Soon after I was finished holding the little guy, they handed me a little girl, taking her out of the isolette for some snuggle time. She was so light, maybe three pounds at the most, but it was amazing to see what a miracle she was. I noticed she was a twin, as her brother was in an isolette on the other side. It looked like he was even smaller. This girl had the longest fingers and a great sucking reflex with her pacifier. It was a privilege to hold such a little one. I was reminded how much God loves each of us and how He made each of us special in His eyes.

See how very much our Father loves us, for he calls us his children,
and that is what we are. But the people who belong to this world don't
recognize that we are God's children because they don't know him.
~ 1 John 3:1 (NLT)

Christine M. Fisher

Be reminded…

> your life is a *miracle* from God.
>
> God's arms are always outstretched ready to *hold* and *embrace* you through every storm.
>
> God breathes His *spirit* into you.
>
> God *loves* you so very much.
>
> you are *special* in God's eyes.
>
> God's *love* and *protection* are with you always.

The eternal God is your refuge, and his everlasting arms are under you.
He drives out the enemy before you; he cries out, "Destroy them."
~ Deuteronomy 33:27 (NLT)

55

Inspirational Living

Do you know anyone who lives a truly inspirational life? By this, I mean their whole life is a true inspiration. The lives that make the greatest impact on me are those who live with physical challenges. Three special people fall into my category of "Inspirational Living."

Veronica

When I was a young teen, I volunteered at a local hospital delivering flowers to patients, working in the coffee shop, and doing various other activities. I helped on a patient floor as well, which is where I met a special lady, Veronica, who was a patient at the hospital for three and half years. When I met Veronica, she had been a quadriplegic for 18 years. I had the blessing of knowing her for about three years before she died.

By the time Veronica was a senior in high school, they discovered she had a disease that caused weakness in her arms and legs. Eventually she was diagnosed with Syringomyelia, which is the growth of tubular cysts in the spinal cord. As the cysts grow in length, the nervous system's messages to various parts of the body weaken and eventually shut off.

When Veronica was 25, she could no longer work due to the progression of the disease. She became paralyzed, except for some movement in her hands. Veronica was able to stay in her parent's home for 18 years. When Veronica was 43, she developed pneumonia. It was decided to permanently move her to a hospital, because the weakened condition of her chest muscles made her susceptible to respiratory infections.

By that time, the disease had claimed the little movement she had in her hands. One of her friends, who was also an electrician at the hospital, blessed her by inventing a device that enabled Veronica to have a control box resting on her chest. In the beginning, there were three controls: one for the television, one for the telephone, and one for the nurse's call button.

Despite being a quadriplegic for 21 years, Veronica's life exemplified many things we can model.

She always had a smile on her face.

She was always positive no matter what her circumstances.

She cared about others, asking about them and their family.

She made people feel special.

She faced life with courage and faith.

What a wonderful example of a grace-filled life. I am blessed to have known her and to call her friend. Her life and example, when I was a young teen, helped shaped me into the person I am today.

Greg and Lilly

It is a distinct honor and privilege to have an inspirational couple in my life, Dr. Gregorio Pedroza and his wife, Lilly. They have three children; their middle child was my husband's best friend while growing up.

In 1981 when Greg was 40, he experienced tingling in his right hand. At that time, there were no MRI's or CAT scans available, so he endured many difficult tests to determine the cause. Greg saw 19 doctors before a physician in New York City discovered he had a tumor at the base of his brain inside the spinal cord. Doctors told Greg if they operated, he would have a 99 percent chance of being a quadriplegic, and if they did not operate, he would have six months to live. The doctor also said if they operated, whatever condition he woke up in would be the way he would remain.

After the diagnosis, Greg returned home and basically slept for a year. It took that long to find a doctor who could operate using high frequency sound rather than a scalpel. They eventually found a doctor in New York City who had performed this procedure on children, but never on an adult.

September 7, 1982 was operation day for Greg. He was in the hospital for two weeks, and then spent three months in rehabilitation. As a result of the surgery, Greg lost the use of his right arm, his balance was not good, and he could walk only with assistance. His left side was left strong, but numb. Greg returned home two months later and endured both chemo and radiation as the tumor was cancerous. On January 11, 1983, Greg returned to his job at IBM as an engineer manager using a scooter, then walker and cane. Greg was able to work for 10 more years before his health challenges forced him to retire.

Because the doctor "unroofed" Greg's spinal cord, he has endured continual, chronic pain 24 hours a day, 7 days a week, for 38 years. This is called Reflex Sympathetic Dystrophy Syndrome, which is characterized by severe non-stop burning pain and extreme sensitivity to touch. "Dante's Inferno," the feeling of constantly being on fire, is a constant in Greg's life. Sleep is the only refuge he gets from this "fire."

A few years ago, Greg and Lilly were at a friend's cottage celebrating the fourth of July. He was pretty much wheelchair bound as his condition was deteriorating even more. He had an unfortunate accident where he hit the back of his head on three steps as he fell while in the wheelchair. This event paralyzed him, but he recovered some use of his left hand from the elbow down. He is now considered a limited functioning quadriplegic who is wheelchair bound.

Greg was sent to a hospital in Syracuse, New York for six weeks, and then to rehabilitation for another six weeks. While there, we visited him, and I gained a greater appreciation for what he and Lilly were going through.

It has been a long road for them. My husband and other friends of Greg have developed and adapted various aids that help him be somewhat independent, allowing him to stay at home.

Through the years, Greg has turned to storytelling and writing. He traveled extensively sharing his stories, laughter and joy. It helps him forget, for a few moments, the constant pain he endures. Throughout the pain and health issues, Greg's life is characterized by service to and love for others. I am always amazed to hear how he is tutoring someone in college, ministering to others who are suffering, calling shut-in's to check on them, writing to inmates in prison, praying for people who send him cards, and the list goes on and on. What a beautiful example of sharing Christ with others no matter the circumstances.

In sharing Greg's story, I must add how much respect I have for his wife, Lilly. She, too, lives an inspirational life, and is upbeat and loving. She supports Greg with his physical needs and has become his hands and feet in keeping their home running. Her patience, unconditional love, and service are exemplary. Her love for cooking is also an inspiration. Shopping, cooking, and cleaning for every meal without complaining is a wonderful thing.

Despite his health challenges and constant pain, Greg's life exemplifies many things we can model.

He is cheerful and has a great smile to share.

He is positive and finds a blessing in everything.

He has a great faith which helps keep him going.

He cares about how others are doing.

He constantly expands his knowledge and learning.

He continues to help others no matter what his physical limitations.

After visiting with Greg and Lilly, I am always blessed, refreshed and inspired. They are wonderful examples of making others feel special, loved, and cared for. They are wonderful inspirations of not allowing anything to stop us from doing what God has called us to. I wish they did not have to suffer, but some day they all will be free of their physical limitations. I am thankful for and blessed by the wonderful lessons Veronica, Greg, and Lilly have taught me by their inspirational lives.

...And we rejoice in the hope of the glory of God. Not only so, but we also rejoice in our sufferings, because we know that suffering produces perseverance; perseverance, character; and character, hope. And hope does not disappoint us, because God has poured out His love into our hearts by the Holy Spirit, whom he has given us.
~ Romans 5:2-5

Christine M. Fisher

56

Mark's Legacy

My heart was saddened when learning that Mark, a gentleman who served with us at the soup kitchen, would not be ministering with us anymore. The Lord called him home. I am happy he is with the Lord, but I will miss Mark's physical presence when we serve at the soup kitchen.

An important thing I can do is remember his legacy and try to live out, to some degree, the example he provided. We all leave a legacy by the way we live. Mark's death hit me hard, maybe because of the ways he touched my heart...

> he shared the Lord through serving drinks (coffee and lemonade) at the soup kitchen.
>
> he gladly served, despite having to sit in a chair with wheels and scooting himself to the refrigerator, coffee maker, and drink area to prep the drinks.
>
> despite not having much money, he would buy coffee or lemonade for the soup kitchen.
>
> he faithfully called to make sure we would pick him up on our soup kitchen day.
>
> he asked about our children if they were not with us.
>
> when we were going to be away on vacation, he called and wished us a good time.
>
> many Thanksgivings and Christmases he called to wish us a nice day.

The last Saturday we worked together, we learned his mother was in a nursing home, so he was living alone. He wanted to be independent, though it was difficult for him. He mentioned he hoped someone would stop by the following Monday and take him to the grocery store, as he was not able to drive. Both my husband and I felt we should offer to take him to the grocery store after the soup kitchen and were thankful he said "yes." We were able to help him out, to be Jesus to him. It was the last time we saw him.

I have one regret. Shortly before he passed, I felt I should call and check on him at Christmas time. I wrote it on my "to do" list, which usually makes me more accountable. However, I failed to do it and missed the opportunity to tell him how much we cared for and loved him. I hope this encourages you to follow up on those little promptings; don't give space for those "one-regrets" to slip in.

I was blessed to work with Mark for 15 years, and I am thankful for the legacy of his sharing the Lord through serving, caring, calling, faithfulness, and giving.

You are missed, Mark. Rest in peace, my dear friend.

His master replied, "Well, done, good and faithful servant...."
~ Matthew 25:23

Christine wearing her stylish hair net while
serving at the soup kitchen.

Christine M. Fisher

57

Always Look for the Helpers

What is there not to like about good ole Mister Rogers? We all know Mister Rogers shared great thoughts and advice, right? I saw a video where his mother shared this thought, "Always look for the helpers...there will always be helpers, even if just on the sidelines. If you look for the helpers, you will know there is hope."

What do you need when...

you are without power for an unknown amount of time?
the land near you is engulfed with uncontrollable fire?
your spouse dies unexpectedly?
a hurricane destroys your house?
you are diagnosed with cancer?
your car is broken, and you have no money for repairs?
your spouse decides to leave you and the family?
your child has an addiction to drugs?
a tornado rips through your area?
someone you know commits suicide?
you have surgery and unsure if it was successful?

Yes, Mister Rogers, your mother was right. When we reflect on any tragedy or catastrophe, we need hope. How do we see hope in our lives despite the tragic events? By looking for helpers, even if they are on the sidelines. Who are these helpers?

Volunteers and agencies who donate time or goods to those in need.
Utility employees who come from different states and work around the clock to restore power.

First responders.

People who donate money to help those hit by tragic events.

People who are willing to give a listening ear to those needing to process their loss.

Nurses and doctors who work extra hours to provide during weather-related emergencies.

People who lift us in prayer.

The one who brings a meal when we are too sick to cook.

Someone willing to give of their time to help rebuild a house damaged or destroyed.

Have you noticed how, during catastrophic events, people are unified and brought together by helping one another? I witnessed this when our area flooded in 2011. People could be seen sharing their supplies, grilling hot dogs to feed others, donating items to those who had nothing, helping others repair their houses, and the list goes on and on. Sometimes these tragedies unite us, and we become stronger.

I encourage you to actively live this out. Who do you know personally going through a difficult time and needs hope? How can you be a helper, even if just on the sidelines, to bring that hope? Have you considered even if you are the one going through a catastrophic event, you might be the hope to someone else?

My eyes were opened to that thought. Having two family members in Florida, one in the path of a hurricane, I texted a friend who also lives in Florida. She shared encouraging, inspiring, faith-filled posts which calmed my fears and helped me center in faith. Despite being in the path of a hurricane, she came off the sidelines to give me hope.

"Always look for the helpers.... there will always be helpers, even if just on the sidelines. If you look for the helpers, you will know there is *hope*."

So do not fear, for I am with you; do not be dismayed, for I am your God.
I will strengthen you and help you; I will uphold
you with my righteous right hand.
~ Isaiah 41:10

58

Mentors

Through the years, I have enjoyed watching *So You Think You Can Dance* on television. I enjoy being graced by the elegance of the dancers and the talent of the choreographers. One season the show featured *The Next Generation* with dancers ages 10 to 14 years old. When the season began, I was not sure I would enjoy watching. It seemed strange to see young kids dancing on the stage. As the shows progressed, I came to appreciate them.

Special bonds were formed between the next generation dancer as they were paired with an "all-star" dancer. Both dancers, the young and the all-star, were of their particular dance genre. The all-star dancer was previously on the show and, in some cases, was the winner of their respective season. What a wonderful opportunity for these next generation dancers to be paired up with an all-star dancer, a special mentor for them.

This pairing allowed the young dancer to...
> learn from the all-star.
> be inspired by the all-star.
> be encouraged by the all-star.
> have someone who believed in them.
> turn to the all-star when they had doubts.
> face and overcome their insecurities.
> have someone to relate to their current experience.
> challenge them to push harder.
> follow the example of the all-star.

The show reminded me of our walk with the Lord. He provides special mentors to walk with us and help us grow in our faith. Can you think of special mentors the Lord has put in your path to help you on your spiritual journey? Have you been blessed to be a special mentor in someone else's life? Either way, mentors are huge blessings.

Who in your life has inspired your walk with the Lord, encouraged and believed in you, challenged you to see things in a different light, or pushed you to do more than you ever thought you could? I encourage you to share with those special mentors what they mean to you and what they have done for you. May you also be blessed by those you have mentored through the years.

Remember your leaders, who spoke the Word of God to you.
Consider the outcome of their way of life and imitate their faith.
Jesus Christ is the same yesterday and today and forever.
~ Hebrews 13:7-8

59

Christ's Reflection

As Christians, we have the responsibility and honor to reflect and be Christ to one another—no matter our age, lot in life, or condition. When we look in the mirror, do we see Christ's reflection? Just as we are all unique and different, so is the form Christ takes in each of us. We are not all meant to reflect Christ in the same way since we all have different gifts. The way I reflect Christ might be completely different from the way you reflect Him. We can learn from each other and maybe stretch ourselves to then reflect Christ in new ways.

It is important to remember that all gifts are equally important. In our humanity, it is easy to think one gift is more important than another. Have you stopped to think about how you see Christ's reflection in others? Or how you reflect Christ to others?

> When I work at the soup kitchen, I see Christ reflected in the people who plan and organize the meal, pick up the food from the food bank, and prepare and serve it. I see Christ reflected in the gentleman who faithfully serves the drinks each month, despite his physical setbacks.

> When I volunteer at school, I see Christ reflected in the teachers who are patient with the students, addressing kindly each child's issues.

> When I go to church, I see Christ reflected in the music minister who has served faithfully in the same position for over 28 years, coordinating and providing worship music.

When I run an errand, I see Christ reflected in the cashier who wishes me a nice day.

When I visit someone who is homebound, I see Christ reflected in the way they stay positive and ask about my family.

When I meet a friend for breakfast, I see Christ reflected in the fact they've cared to keep in touch.

When I reach out to a friend for prayer, I see Christ reflected when I know they are praying.

When I ask my editor or friend for feedback, I see Christ reflected when they give constructive input to help my thoughts come together even better.

Have you ever visited someone to reflect Christ to them, and you saw Christ reflected through them? How is it they ministered to you simply through their attitude or their outlook with their situation? I am always blessed in seeing Christ reflected in those I minister to…they truly reflect Christ through their life and example.

There is only one Christ who works through us in different ways, reflecting Him to all we meet, if we allow Him. We are each needed to complete the body of Christ and reflect Him in all we do.

And we, who with unveiled faces all reflect the Lord's glory,
are being transformed into his likeness with ever-increasing
glory, which comes from the Lord, who is the Spirit.
~ 2 Corinthians 3:18

60

Learning People's Stories

God made each of us unique, thus we each have our own stories that make us God's special creation. He is the potter and we are the clay. He molds and shapes our lives in different ways. Each of us is His masterpiece with no two being alike.

It is interesting to listen to people's stories. On a Christian music cruise, I had the opportunity to meet many people from all walks of life, each with different experiences and various backgrounds. God put special people in my path; usually one person each day.

GOD IS THE HEALER

The first night of our cruise, we sat with three couples we had not met. While some of the people were talking about their dogs, one gentleman, in passing, quickly said something about getting a dog around the time his wife had a brain tumor. His statement piqued my interest, though I kept debating whether to bring up the topic. Finally, I asked the couple about it, hoping I heard him correctly. Indeed, I was excited to hear her story.

In early 2014, she had an image taken of the inside of her eye, at which point the doctors saw a tumor. The brain tumor was removed and, thankfully, was non-cancerous. She could not walk for nine months due to infections that left her with long hospital stays and great weight loss. The couple battled through the days and months. The dog kept her company during those difficult days. She was excited to be helping at a day mission trip on the cruise. As she said, "God still has things for me to do and I am ready." To look at her, one would never know she had been through so much.

What a blessing to hear her story from just a quick, passing comment her husband made at dinner. God sure is awesome.

GOD IS ALWAYS WITH US, GUIDING US

The following day, I ran into a couple I met the previous year on the cruise. We were looking for a table for lunch and decided to sit with a lady eating alone. She had encouraging stories of God's goodness as He helped her make it through difficult circumstances. As a veteran, she has endured several health issues, yet her faith in God and His goodness shone forth.

GOD IS FAITHFUL, HOLD ONTO HIS PROMISES

That evening I recognized another couple from the cruise the previous year. I remembered we ate dinner together and enjoyed a beautiful sunset from our table. What a God moment that was…from all the people on the cruise, there we were next to each other again. The wife asked how my year had been and she shared some heartache they experienced shortly after returning home from the cruise. It had been a challenging year for them, but they remained steadfast in their faith.

GOD PROVIDES FOR THE NEEDY

The following night I enjoyed a conversation with another woman. She and her husband live a short distance from us and have a connection to a pizza place in their city. I learned that, on Friday nights, they take pizza to the homeless. What a wonderful ministry to deliver food to the homeless. They have expanded their ministry to include toiletries and clothing, as well as bringing other people into the ministry.

GOD IS IN THE MIRACLE BUSINESS

As only God can orchestrate, the last morning at breakfast, we sat with a couple and a family of four. What are the chances the two women were nurses? One of the nurses worked in Labor and Delivery, so I was able to share my story of volunteering in the NICU. They both thanked me for loving the littlest of ones who need extra tender love and care, as they know the importance. One of the girls, a senior in high school, was a twin. How wonderful to learn the twins were born at less than two pounds each. Today, they are healthy and strong with no developmental delays of any kind. What a blessing the NICU was available for them.

May these thoughts encourage you to engage with people, to learn their stories, and find out why they are like they are. We are all important in God's kingdom on earth. We each have different gifts and talents, yet we can show respect and share the love of Christ with those we meet.

Continue to glorify God with your life and share your story with others. You are an important part of the kingdom of God.

Jesus said, "Go home to your own people and tell them how much the Lord has done for you, and how he has had mercy on you."
- Mark 5:19

Christine M. Fisher

61

The Symphony of Life

You are a part of a grand symphony – the symphony of life.

As I listened to my daughter's last college wind ensemble performance, my thoughts pondered how playing in a symphony can be symbolic of our relationship with the Lord.

With so many different instruments in a symphony, the conductor has the arduous job of making sure each section comes in at the precise moment in order to make the music sound just right. What is key for the conductor in making this happen? The instrumentalists must always maintain focus on the conductor; glancing between the music and the conductor's cues. What a great parallel for us in our relationship with the Lord.

God is the Master Conductor in this symphony of life.

Just as the conductor is in charge of all the instruments, so God conducts and orchestrates the entire world. His arms are outstretched encompassing everything just as the conductor does for all involved in the symphony. We need to continually keep our eyes and focus on our Creator, our Lord, paying attention to His leading, His cues, His word, His presence.

**The Holy Spirit leads and guides us
when we keep our eyes fixed on Him.
Are you in "tune" with the Creator?**

For each performance, the musicians are given pieces of music to study and practice for days on end, and then perform with the symphony. Isn't this a parallel for our lives? Each day is like a piece of music we perform.

We learn from our mistakes, study His word to guide us, glorify Him, love Him and others and live to the best of our ability.

There are several instruments in a wind ensemble, ranging from the piccolo, to the clarinet, to the bassoon, to the various saxophones, to the trombones, to name a few. Each instrument has its own unique and special sound. God made each of us, His instruments, unique and special with gifts and talents of our own. God does not have a favorite "instrument." No gift or talent ranks above another. God loves each of us infinitely just as we are.

Think about how the members of the ensemble first practice their parts alone, hold sectional rehearsals followed by the whole symphony combining to make beautiful music, each performing their special part. We are parts of different groups of people, our families, those we work with, volunteer with, and socialize with. We reach out to these people, touching them, blessing them, and helping make beautiful music together following our Conductor.

I encourage you…
> keep your eyes on the Master Conductor.
> be His instrument and make beautiful music with your life.
> be in tune with the Grand Symphony.

For we are God's masterpiece. He has created us anew in Christ Jesus,
so we can do the good things he planned for us long ago.
~ Ephesians 2:10 (NLT)

62

God's Grace

God's grace ~ a thought that occurred to me one day as I was thanking God for His goodness. In researching different definitions about the word grace, I found two which are applicable: favor, kindness, friendship; gifts freely bestowed by God, as miracles, prophecy, tongues.

There was a time I personally experienced God's grace in a mighty way; a time when He extended His favor and performed a "miracle."

Saturday started with the blessing of holding little ones in the NICU. Then I headed to church, where I would arrive early, giving me extra time to pray.

As I drove down the highway, I noticed two cars further ahead swerving from one lane to the next. I thought perhaps there was a slower car ahead of them not visible to me. Suddenly, the car directly in front of me swerved and headed toward the shoulder of the road. As it swerved, I could see the problem. A huge cardboard box was standing in the middle of our lane. Without thinking, I swerved to miss the box. Instead of going to the shoulder where the other car was, I stayed closer to the middle of the road and eventually, I think with my eyes closed, moved into the passing lane. It happened so fast I did not even have time to see if the passing lane was clear. I have never experienced going from 65 mph to swerving to avoid an accident. I saw God's grace as He granted favor and kindness in guiding me to safety. I believe it was a miracle, as things could have ended very differently.

Just ahead, I saw a pickup truck on the shoulder with a washing machine in the back. It seems the box must have blown off. I kept saying, "Thank you, Lord. Thank you for your grace." I repeated that prayer all the way to church. I am thankful the other drivers were also safe by God's grace; God's angels protected us.

I continued to receive God's grace that day. During the evening church service, it was powerful to see the light from the sunset beaming through the stained glass windows. I could not pull my eyes away, and it was so bright I needed sunglasses. Oddly enough, I later realized the sun coming through the windows was only visible from the exact spot I was sitting.

Following the service, there was a gathering for dinner and a movie. After the movie, a friend came to talk to me. He said that seeing me serve during the church dinner blessed and calmed him, as he was apprehensive about attending. He also shared a story about his daughter; a story that gave me chills. She was recently diagnosed with a carotid artery tear and sent home with medications and to rest. The severity of her condition was underestimated by the doctors. Some friends came to visit and one, a nurse, realized his daughter was in trouble, called an ambulance, and his daughter was immediately admitted to the ICU. The next day an angioplasty was performed. When the doctors inserted the balloon, her artery totally collapsed, and she had a seizure. The surgeon saved her life while she was on the operating table. She was thankful to be alive and learned to adjust to her new life. He added, "The doctor said if this had not happened when it did, she would have died within six months."

When he finished sharing his story, I felt I needed to share my story of the trip to church that day. He truly understood the magnitude of what happened and agreed it was a miracle I was standing there; we exchanged hugs because we were both grateful for God's grace. I felt the Lord hugging me through that encounter. As my friend said later, that night was "a spiritual joining of two sincere hearts." I could not agree more, and I am so grateful.

Later as I was praying for my friend, his daughter and family, God's grace resonated in my heart. Yes, God's grace, His favor, kindness, miracle, with His perfect timing, led to those events happening, as difficult as they were. God's grace spared her life throughout the procedure saving her from something worse which could have led to immediate death. I emailed him later to share the thought with him; God's grace at its finest.

I also shared the blessing of the sun shining on me through the stained glass window that Saturday night. He encouraged me, "I believe that was God telling you His light was shining on you; saving you from harm, so you can continue to inspire others through your writing." This gentleman is a great supporter of my weekly thoughts and one who has encouraged me to pursue compiling them into a book. As a matter of fact, he has written the Foreword for this book.

I continue to be thankful for God's grace. What great memories and miracles to reflect on. Can you think of some ways you have experienced God's grace in your life?

For he will command his angels concerning
you to guard you in all your ways.
On their hands they will bear you up,
lest you strike your foot against a stone.
~ Psalm 91:11-12 (ESV)

63

Adversity

My youngest son accompanied my husband and me to a social gathering. We sat at a table near a woman in a wheelchair and overheard her inviting people to participate in a Big Ball tournament the following weekend. ("Big Ball" is similar to softball but uses a bigger, softer 16" ball.) This is an annual benefit that helps her with medical costs. My son, the baseball enthusiast, told me he would love to play. The next weekend, while watching my son play three Big Ball games, I had the blessing of talking with this woman, her father, mother and step-father. They are all wonderful examples of overcoming adversity and making the best of it.

When I am at events like these, I find myself blessed and in awe of those who live through great adversity, and I find myself praying for them. Imagine what it must be like to…

> be paralyzed for eight years.
> not have use of your arms, hands, or legs.
> not be able to walk.
> be told you would never drive.
> not be defeated by your situation.

This woman, through lots of determination and perseverance, rather than stubbornness (the word her father used), regained the use of both arms and hands. She was determined to drive again, and now drives herself to medical appointments, three hours each way, four times a month. She set a goal for walking again one day, and I believe she will. What an inspiration and example for not letting adversity get her down. It is pure joy to talk with her, to hear her positive outlook on life and to see her overcome so many obstacles with a wonderful and peaceful attitude.

Christine M. Fisher

I smiled a few times as the woman's mom wondered who the second baseman was. I was a little hesitant to say he was my son, since I was not sure whether she would say something good or bad. She said, "He is good." (I breathed a sigh of relief.) At the Sunday event, the woman's step-dad introduced himself and said, "You have a fine young man there."

All this also made me think about adversity…

> maybe you are an athlete and lose almost every game you play.
> maybe you have cancer or some other chronic illness.
> maybe you have a loved one serving in the military who is deployed.
> maybe your spouse died unexpectedly.
> maybe you are trying to find someplace to live.
> maybe you are unemployed and need to find a job.
> maybe your child has an addiction.

Through all these things, our attitude and perspective are vital in how we handle situations. We can dwell on the negative and let it defeat us, or we can choose to dwell on the positive and work to overcome our situation one-step at a time. As this woman often reminds herself, there is always someone worse off.

I encourage you to take that first step to overcome whatever adversity you are facing. Try to reach out to another for encouragement or help. And remember you are not alone. God is with you through it all.

…And surely I am with you always, to the very end of the age.
~ Matthew 28:20

64

I Cherish You

I have always longed to have a surprise party given in my honor. Not because I wanted to feel "important," but because I wanted to know people were coming together to celebrate "the me" God made. The longing started many years ago when some friends had surprise birthday dinners. I thought how special that would be. My husband says he could never pull off a surprise party because I would figure it out; I'm just too smart. He suggested a "make your own sundae" gathering at a park. I think my wanting a birthday gathering was a ripple effect of having a high school graduation party for my youngest son and having an empty nest.

The invitation said, "I just want your presence not presents. If you feel inclined to, you can give me a word of encouragement or tell me something you "love" about me." (I wondered later if that was a little too presumptuous.) Much to my surprise, it was great to hear people say it was a nice idea to have a celebration like this. (Maybe it was the sundae they were really referring to.)

It was a beautiful sunny evening, and the park was a great gathering place. About 30 people came to the "celebrate Christine" get-together. People came to truly celebrate me, and I felt extra special. It was humbling when, at one point, everyone started singing Happy Birthday. It helped me realize, once again, how my life matters; just a simple, ordinary gal, trying to live day by day for the Lord, blessing others in whatever way I can.

People I worked with over the years joined the celebration as well as people I had not seen in a few years; there were church people, friends and family who came together in fellowship. Everyone was getting to know others and enjoying the evening. As I made the rounds, it was wonderful to see how the guests who did not know each other were conversing. Many of my family and friends also knew others who were there. The saying, "it is a small world" proved true.

My favorite part was people's willingness to share something special about how I have touched their life. Many wrote touching messages in cards and others wrote a note on a poster board we had available. One friend brought a bouquet of flowers with a card saying, "I cherish you." Later that evening, as I opened the envelopes one by one, tears came to my eyes as I read each note. What a blessing to read how my life has impacted others because of Christ in me. Even a few people who could not attend took time to email what they love about me.

Isn't it important to share with others the impact they have on our lives? We are all valuable and contribute to this world. Yes, each of our lives matter and each of us have a purpose in God's master plan.

The words "I cherish you" also made me think how God cherishes each of us. Doesn't He let us know how much He loves us daily? From the beautiful creation He made for us to enjoy to the family and friends He has placed in our path to share life with. He continually lets us know of His great love for us and how He cherishes us. He even sent His only Son to die for us.

As I thought more about that special evening, it occurred to me how perfect the card accompanying the saying, "I cherish you" was reflected in my life that night. It rang true as I thought about each person who came to enrich my birthday celebration.

> *Cherish* every memory.
> *Love* every moment.
> *Embrace* every possibility.

Yes, indeed, I do *cherish* every conversation and contact from my birthday celebration, forever etched in my memory. I do *love* every moment when others celebrated Christ in me, and I am so thankful I *embraced* the possibility of celebrating me and am so thankful for all who *embraced* me.

As you go about life keep this saying in mind....
Cherish every memory. *Love* every moment. *Embrace* every possibility.

Remember to let people know how much you love them and be sure to celebrate the specialness they bring to your life.

For you created my inmost being; you knit me together in my mother's womb. I praise you because I am fearfully and wonderfully made; your works are wonderful, I know that full well.
~ Psalm 139:13-14

65

Loving Memories

The Lord places special people in our path, whether it be members of our family, close friends or acquaintances. Lessons can be learned from each one—every person is unique and has something to offer. The hardest part of losing loved ones is the pain and loneliness of those left behind, even if the person was a Christian. We should keep their spirit alive through our loving memories of them.

As I reflect on two special people in my life, maybe you, too, can identify with some of the following thoughts, and reflect on special people who have gone before you. I am filled with joy and happiness in knowing my Grandma Palmiter and Great-Aunt Hazel are spending eternity with God. I have comfort in this fact since they proclaimed Jesus Christ as their Lord while on this earth and their lives confirmed this. Knowing they are no longer suffering and in pain is a blessing and a prayer now answered. I look forward to the day when their bodies will be transformed into the likeness and image of God.

The memories of past years together are such a treasure that is indeed hard to measure. I will always hold close to my heart the memories of the Sunday dinners, games and outings, as well as listening to the music played to Jesus on the organ.

My most important memories are the way they lived their lives.

Faith in Jesus is most important—He is always with us and will help us.

Whatever happens in life, we need to make the best of it without complaining.

Our lives can be made happier in knowing we helped someone–no matter how small the need.

By truly listening to someone–whether an acquaintance or a stranger–we can ease their burdens.

Having a good laugh every day is healthy.

I thank the Lord for both my grandma and great-aunt, and the inspiration their lives are to me. They certainly helped me grow closer to the Lord and become a better person.

The memory of the righteous will be a blessing,
but the name of the wicked will rot.
~ Proverbs 10:7

66

God's Miraculous Power

Miracles and healings still happen today. I am excited to share a current day healing of my friend, Ken. He has experienced health issues through the years, with three major healings or miracles.

When Ken was a child, he contracted polio which left him with pain in his legs. He was also born with a birth defect in his lower spine. Because of these issues, he could not walk normally. Back surgery in the 1980s did not give him much improvement. Sometime after the back surgery, a couple with the gift of healing visited his church. They laid hands on Ken and prayed for his healing. Immediately the pain in his back and legs went away and he was able to walk normally, though he never told them what was ailing him. What a healing from God.

Ken has also endured heart issues through the years. Driving along the highway one day, he saw a car pulled over with a flat tire. Seeing a lady with two babies inside the car, he stopped to offer his assistance. As he was changing the tire, he did not feel well and was not able to properly respond to the lady talking with him. He knew he had to get her back on the road, so he tried to work quickly. Once the lady was on her way, Ken drove to the closest gas station, reclined his seat and waited until he felt better. (This was before the days of cell phones.) When he went to the doctor a few days later, he learned he had suffered a heart attack, had a 95 percent blockage, and eventually had surgery. What a miracle he was able to help another while having a heart attack himself.

Ken has also struggled with stomach issues. He went to several doctors but was unable to get a diagnosis for quite a while. After a CT scan, the results showed he had a condition called gastroparesis, which is where the stomach has smooth muscle and no ridges needed to digest the food. There is no known cure for this condition, so Ken made an appointment to go to a specialized hospital to have an internal pacemaker inserted in his stomach.

The Sunday before surgery, Ken's pastor preached on Luke 8:43-48. This is the story of the woman who had a bleeding problem that had defied doctors for many years. As Jesus passed by, the woman knew if she could only touch His garment, she would be healed. At the end of the sermon, the pastor invited people who needed healing to close their eyes and to reach out and touch the hem of Jesus' garment. When Ken did that, he had a severe pain in his stomach and then the pain subsided. Ken started feeling better. That night he could not sleep. He did not say anything to anyone for a few days because Satan was planting seeds of doubt as to whether he was really healed. The day before surgery, Ken cancelled his appointment for the internal pacemaker. He has not experienced stomach pain since the healing.

Ken recently shared this story with his church family to edify the body of Christ and glorify God. He said, "Some may ask why are you sharing this now? Well I don't have an explanation (as to why I don't have any stomach issues) and neither do my doctors. Sometimes the answer is from above. Two thousand years ago Jesus walked this earth healing everyone who asked, and he is still healing people today. All you need to do is ask and believe."

As I talked with Ken, he said he did not deserve the healing. Isn't it true that none of us "deserve" any of the good things God gives us, especially the gift of salvation? God, in His infinite goodness, freely gives us these gifts because of His love, mercy, and grace. Sometimes it is hard to understand how God works, why He heals one person and not another, or why the woman with the issue of blood had to suffer for twelve years before her healing. We must trust God, continue to seek Him, and glorify Him. He is a good, good God.

O Lord my God, I called to you for help, and you healed me.
~ Psalm 30:2

67

Community

While attending a weekend retreat, I talked briefly with a woman about church "community," where Christian people support each other, especially through the tough times. A place that is safe and secure, like the saying, "What happens in Vegas stays in Vegas."

I often hear about the importance of having older, wiser mentors in our lives as well as the importance of mentoring younger people. Yes, community. Sometimes I feel this is lacking in my life, as I am not part of a small group where community support is the greatest. Other times, I think I have community support with friends who are older, more experienced and wiser, which blesses me. On the flip side, I hope I can lend encouragement and prayerful support to the younger people in my life. These cases are most often one on one with people. I think that also constitutes community support.

Often our schedules are so hurried we do not make time to be in community. We are too busy or too preoccupied with ourselves to be available for one more person. To be community, we must be able to trust people in order to be vulnerable, which can be a scary thing.

Right after the conversation about church "community," I went outside for another view of the lake, which was quiet, calm and peaceful. Suddenly, at the far end of the lake, I heard ducks making noise. Much to my surprise, I saw a parade of ducks, reminding me of the importance of community. I could not believe the line of ducks kept growing. Yes, God's perfect timing.

As I drew close to the main building, I was shocked to see a lone puzzle piece on the wet pavement. What was this puzzle piece doing in the middle of the walkway? It reminded me how we are all an important piece in the puzzle of community for others.

In retrospect, I find it interesting the woman I spoke to at the retreat was "community" for me when I tried my hand at archery. She was kind enough to jump in and help direct my technique, as she had experience. I appreciated the community spirit to help and cheer for me when I hit the target.

Interestingly, I experienced two community outreaches the next week. The first was from a couple who emailed me because they noticed my husband and I were not at Bible Study (we had an unexpected commitment). Their simple email brightened my day and made me feel part of a community who cared enough to let us know we were missed and hoped to see us the following week.

The second instance was when I went to pick up a DVD from our Bible study group so we could view it at home. The lady invited me to come in, sit and talk. She wanted the update on my family and life as we both attended the same church about 18 years earlier. We had not had a chance to converse during Bible study. An hour flew by, and I left feeling a sense of community.

I encourage you to look for ways, even little ways, you can be community for others. We can build our community, one person at a time.

Ready, set, go…be community.

"For where two or three are gathered in my name, there am I among them." ~ Matthew 18:20

68

Influences

It was bittersweet when the time came for my last child to embark on his exciting college years. Through a series of events on his last official day at home, I started thinking about the theme of "influences."

Aren't there so many influences in our lives that can be both positive or negative? There are addictions ranging from drugs to alcohol, to hoarding, to eating excessively. The world tells us we should be chasing money and fame. We hear it is okay to lie and cheat to make it to the top. Another lie is we need to be the best at everything we do because climbing the corporate ladder is most important.

What positive influences are in our lives? People who encourage us when we are going through a tough time. People who lift us in prayer without our asking, or who send a friendly note to say they are thinking of us. Christian music that ministers to our soul and sermons that speak to our heart. How powerful are even the small things we do, knowing we can influence someone or something? Isn't that awesome to think about?

To make my son's last evening at home special, we wanted to take him to one of his favorite restaurants. Knowing my son has grown in his relationship with the Lord because of the influence of two Young Life leaders, we invited them along. After dinner, my husband started a prayer for our son, and the leaders joined in. My prayer was letting out tears. It was a treasured moment with precious heartfelt love.

Earlier in the afternoon, my son was looking up the phone number of one of his school monitors. He called and they arranged to meet for ice cream later in the evening. I thought it was special he wanted to see her one more time before he left for college. My son had told me about her sometime during his senior year of high school. He would stay later at school in order to talk with her. He was able to confide in her and not be judged. This woman is a Christian and would tell my son she was praying for him. As a mom, I was touched. I sent her a booklet of verses I had penned years earlier and wrote a note letting her know how much I appreciated her listening to and praying for him.

When they met for ice cream, I was able to join them so I could personally thank her for being present in my son's life. It truly was a joy to meet this 74-year-old woman. What wonderful wisdom and encouragement she offered my son. We exchanged hugs, she prayed over my son, and ended with saying, "Peace be with you."

Indeed, our lives have great influence on others. Each of us have opportunities throughout the day, each day. Take a minute to reflect. Who has influenced your life? Whose life have you influenced? We might not fully know the answer to either of these questions until we get to heaven and everything is revealed. How many times do we pray for people without their knowledge? However, God certainly knows, and I am sure He smiles when we do. When we pray, often the outcome is different because of our prayers. Prayer influences our lives in ways we do not even know.

Think about the things you do, the influence you might have in someone's life. Do you treat life with respect? Do you treat everyone you meet with respect? Go change the world with your influence.

Let us think of ways to motivate one another to acts of love and good works. And let us not neglect our meeting together, as some people do, but encourage one another, especially now that the day of his return is drawing near.
~ Hebrews 10:24-25 (NLT)

Section 4

GOD'S PRESENCE ILLUMINATED IN JESUS

For God so loved the world that he gave his one and only Son,
that whoever believes in him shall not perish but have eternal life.
~ John 3:16

God's plan for salvation began with sending Jesus to earth as a baby, His one and only Son. Jesus was divine, yet God sent Him to be in "human-form," so all would be able to relate even more deeply to Jesus.

After 33 years, Jesus was put to death on a cross for our sins. He rose three days later and walked this earth for another 50 days before ascending back to heaven.

God loved you and me so much that He sent Jesus to earth. God wants us all in heaven one day with Him and Jesus is the way to get there.

God's presence illuminated in Jesus.

69

Emmanuel

Advent and Christmas are special times filled with rich meaning. An important thought that resonates with me is *Emmanuel,* which means, "God with us." This is truly what we celebrate at Christmas, Jesus' birth, God *with* us.

Jesus was known by several names. What an amazing thing to see the different roles Jesus has, the ways we can relate to Him. Take a few minutes to read these names of Jesus and the scripture verses. Let them sink into your very being.

SON OF GOD
And the angel answered her, "The Holy Spirit will come upon you,
and the power of the Most High will overshadow you; therefore
the child to be born will be called holy—the Son of God."
~ Luke 1:35 (ESV)

SON OF THE MOST HIGH
He will be great and will be called the Son of the Most High.
The Lord God will give him the throne of his father David.
~ Luke 1:32

SON OF MAN
"For the Son of Man came to seek and to save the lost."
~ Luke 19:10 (ESV)

GOOD SHEPHERD
"I am the good shepherd. The good shepherd lays down his life for the sheep."
~ John 10:11

LAMB OF GOD

As Jesus walked by, John looked at him and declared,
"Look! There is the Lamb of God!"
~ John 1:36 (NLT)

KING OF THE JEWS

Pilate asked Jesus, "Are you the king of the Jews?"
Jesus replied, "You have said it."
~ Mark 15:2 (NLT)

LIVING CORNERSTONE

You are coming to Christ, who is the living cornerstone of God's temple.
He was rejected by people, but he was chosen by God for great honor.
~ 1 Peter 2:4 (NLT)

BREAD OF LIFE

Jesus said to them, "I am the bread of life;
whoever comes to me shall not hunger,
and whoever believes in me shall never thirst."
~ John 6:35 (ESV)

ALPHA AND OMEGA

I am the Alpha and the Omega, the First and
the Last, the Beginning and the End.
~ Revelation 22:13

THE ROOT, OFFSPRING OF DAVID, MORNING STAR

"I, Jesus, have sent my angel to give you this testimony for the churches.
I am the Root and the Offspring of David, and the bright Morning Star."
~ Revelation 22:16

Back to the first name: EMMANUEL–God *with* us. This birth of Jesus, God *with* us, truly the most meaningful event in all history was foreshadowed in the Old Testament and confirmed in the New Testament:

Therefore the Lord himself will give you a sign:
The virgin will conceive and give birth to a
son, and will call him Emmanuel.
~ Isaiah 7:14

"The virgin will conceive and give birth to a son,
and they will call him Emmanuel"
(which means "God with us").
~ Matthew 1:23

Jesus is the most important gift of all time. I am thankful God sent His only Son to earth to enable us the privilege of spending eternity with God, if we accept Jesus as our Lord and Savior.

For God so loved the world that he gave his one and only Son,
that whoever believes in him shall not perish but have eternal life.
~ John 3:16

God the Father, Jesus the Son, the Holy Spirit: Three separate persons yet one; the Trinity. Jesus the Son came to earth to be a human so we can relate to God the Father; God *with* us. Jesus willingly died for you and me in order to leave us the gift of His Spirit, which also remains with us.

Nevertheless, I tell you the truth: it is to your advantage
that I go away, for if I do not go away, the Helper will not
come to you. But if I go, I will send him to you.
~ John 16:7 (ESV)

Do you live differently *knowing* that Jesus truly is Emmanuel–God *with* you? Do you see God *with* you…

    in the daily struggles?

    in the midst of heartache?

    in the joy of good times?

    in the loneliness?

in the storms of life?

in the hard decisions you wrestle with?

in the anxiety you try to control?

in the success you encountered with a difficult task?

Be assured, no matter what: EMMANUEL–God is *with* you. He watches over everything. Nothing will happen to you that He does not already know and that He will not experience with you.

Ponder for a few minutes Jesus' entrance into this world. It was a rough, bumpy ride to finally get to Bethlehem. He was born in a stable, placed in a manger, which was a feeding trough for the animals. Jesus was beaten and died on a cross. God did not spare His only Son from going through hardship, yet His Father was always with Him.

EMMANUEL–God *with* us–provides the same comfort for you and me.

Teach these new disciples to obey all the commands I have given you.
And be sure of this: I am with you always, even to the end of the age.
~ Matthew 28:20 (NLT)

70

The Lenten Season

In life, it is good to take time to reflect on our journey and the changes we can make to improve. The season of Lent (a period of forty days before Easter) provides an opportunity to refocus the direction we are headed. However, we certainly do not need to wait until Lent to make the changes we feel are necessary. Anytime we are inspired to change is a great time to begin anew.

Are there changes you can make to improve and deepen your relationship with the Lord? Are there changes you can make to help you be a better you? Would reflecting on Jesus' sacrifice make you more thankful? Some ways to help us refocus are:

> fasting,
> repenting of our sins,
> spiritual discipline—praying, reading scripture,
> almsgiving.

Christ fasted. He took time to pray to His Father. He helped the poor. If Christ did these things, shouldn't we do these same things? Participating in these actions will not get us into heaven; they are more a by-product to enhance our relationship with Christ. Our salvation is based on our acceptance of Christ as our Savior.

I love celebrating the holiest of days reflecting on the events of Holy Thursday, Good Friday, and Easter, which are the pinnacles of our faith. On Holy Thursday, we can relive the Last Supper, where Jesus sacrificed Himself. That night He also washed His disciples' feet as an act of being a humble servant. He commands us to do the same. On Good Friday, we think about Jesus carrying the cross, feeling the agony He endured for us. On Easter Sunday, He rose and was victorious over sin and death in order to set us free.

Being Christians means sharing in Jesus' resurrection and the joy that comes with knowing He paid the ultimate price for our salvation. We have the privilege of proclaiming and sharing Him with all we meet. Knowing we are filled with the Holy Spirit, who is always present to encourage and give us power, is comforting.

Jesus said to her (Martha), "I am the resurrection and the life.
He who believes in me will live, even though he dies;
and whoever lives and believes in me will never die. Do you believe this?"
~ John 11:25-26

Christine M. Fisher

71

The Cross

One of the best known symbols of Christianity is the *cross*. What a great sacrifice Jesus made to save mankind through His painful, agonizing death, which is hard to fathom since people in our society are not crucified. Reading stories of what Jesus went through helps us appreciate the torment He suffered for our salvation (Matthew 27:28-31).

What does the cross represent for you and me?
> Goodness conquered evil.
>> Satan is defeated.
>>> Salvation for all our sins.
>>>> Victory over sin and death.

> *The sting of death is sin, and the power of sin*
> *is the law. But thanks be to God.*
> *He gives us the victory through our Lord Jesus Christ.*
> ~ 1 Corinthians 15:56-57

What did the cross represent for Jesus?
> Great suffering.
>> The ultimate sacrifice for mankind.
>>> Obedience to God's plan.

> *"Father, if you are willing, take this cup from me;*
> *yet not my will, but yours be done."*
> ~ Luke 22:42

What did the cross represent for Mary?

Sorrow seeing her son suffer.

Her seed crushing the serpent's head.

God's plan was fulfilled at last.

*Blessed is she who has believed that what the Lord
has said to her will be accomplished.*
~ Luke 1:45

What did the cross represent to Satan?

He was not in charge anymore.

He was defeated.

God has the victory.

*He replied, "I saw Satan fall like lightning from heaven. I have
given you authority to trample on snakes and scorpions and to
overcome all the power of the enemy; nothing will harm you."*
~ Luke 10:18-19

What other gifts are lavished upon us by Jesus' drops of blood that He
shed on the cross for you and me?

Forgiveness

Mercy

Grace

Everlasting love

Peace

Joy

*In him we have redemption through his blood, the forgiveness
of sins, in accordance with the riches of God's grace that he
lavished on us with all wisdom and understanding.*
~ Ephesians 1:7-8

72

The Jesse Tree

One December day we had icy conditions followed by snow. My husband was in the kitchen when he heard a loud noise. He opened the side door to peer into the garage and saw a pine branch sticking through the roof. As this happened in December and I was in the Christmas frame of mind, a scripture about "Jesse's tree" came to mind.

> *A shoot will come up from the stump of Jesse; from*
> *his roots a Branch will bear fruit.*
> ~ Isaiah 11:1

With God's perfect timing, Isaiah 11:1 was read that weekend at church. The sermon's focus was on "spiritual fruit" in our lives. I believe an accurate rephrasing of this verse is:

> *"From the Messiah, Jesus (a shoot) will grow from the lineage*
> *(stump) of Jesse (King David's father). From the roots of Jesse,*
> *Jesus (a Branch) will carry out God's will (bear fruit)."*

There was not a physical "Jesse tree" when Isaiah wrote the verse, but the symbolism was a good parallel, especially when a "Jesse tree" appeared in our garage.

My husband posted a few pictures of the fallen tree on social media. A friend immediately responded, asking if we needed help removing the branch or fixing the roof. His family lost everything in the flood of 2011 and our family has reached out to support them through the years. He wanted to return the favor. As we met to discuss the repairs, he shared this story.

His daughter was turning 17-years-old that month and wanted to talk to him about her birthday. He wondered what she wanted and how much money it would entail. He was pleasantly surprised to learn she wanted to help others rather than personally receive presents. She said, "Dad, I have everything I need and would rather help others, but I want to do it secretly." Through her generosity, his daughter was able to bless a single mom with two children. He added, "Even though she was only 9-years-old when the area flooded, she remembers people helping us in our time of need. Your family has been a great influence in her life."

I could not help but think back to the branch that suddenly appeared through our garage roof, and how we were hearing about a teen wanting to bless others, to produce "fruit." She remembered being helped when they had absolutely nothing. Maybe that tree branch came through our roof so this friend could share the story with us. His daughter's life was now producing the fruit of kindness and goodness.

Think about spiritual fruit in your life. The fruit that changes your outlook, the way you interact with others, and the way you view others. The fruit of sharing love, joy, peace, patience, kindness, goodness, faithfulness, gentleness and self-control. The fruit of seeking out those who need help, sharing your time and talents with others. How do you share that spiritual fruit with others daily?

Jesus came into the world to spread the Good News. Our lives need to bear spiritual fruit to show our experience of truly knowing Jesus in our hearts and living moment by moment for Him.

In that day the Branch of the Lord
will be beautiful and glorious,
and the fruit of the land will be the pride
and glory of the survivors in Israel.
~ Isaiah 4:2

Christine M. Fisher

73

I am Barabbas

At a Good Friday service, I was reminded of Barabbas. He is a person mentioned in all four Gospels who has an interesting parallel to our lives. I encourage you to read Luke 23:13-25.

What do we know about Barabbas? Not a whole lot, but enough to see his significance. Barabbas was thrown into prison for insurrection, an organized opposition to the Roman authorities. He was also a robber and murderer. He was guilty of sin and wrongdoing. He was condemned, awaiting his death sentence by crucifixion. He was in the right place at the right time since one prisoner could be released and set free. Barabbas' name was Jesus Barabbas. Barabbas in Aramaic, bar abba, translates to "Son of the Father."

At the time for Barabbas to be crucified, Jesus was brought before the Roman governor, Pilate, accused of being the "Son of God, the King of the Jews." Pilate said to the Jews, "I find no basis for a charge against him. But it is your custom for me to release to you one prisoner at the time of Passover." Then he asked, "Who do you want me to release?" The Jews shouted back, "Barabbas. Give us Barabbas."

> Jesus was unjustly sentenced to die a criminal's death for no wrongdoing.
> Jesus died in place of Barabbas.
> Barabbas was set free because Jesus took his place on the cross.

HAVE YOU EVER THOUGHT OF YOURSELF AS "BARABBAS"?

Reflect on that thought and all it means. You, born into sin, stood condemned until Jesus stepped in and set you free from bondage. Jesus took your place on the cross. In God's plan of salvation, Jesus, a man who did no wrong, died. Just as Barabbas' name means, Son of the Father, you and I are sons (and daughters) of the Father because of Jesus.

YES, I AM BARABBAS.

How symbolic that Barabbas, meaning "Son of the Father," was set free because of Jesus Christ, the true "Son of the Father." Yes, Jesus is truly the Son of God.

See how very much our Father loves us, for he calls us his children,
and that is what we are. But the people who belong to this world don't
recognize that we are God's children because they don't know him.
~ 1 John 3:1 (NLT)

74

The Humanity of Jesus

One Easter it occurred to me how Jesus Christ, while on this earth, experienced the same basic human emotions and feelings as you and me. He is divine, being God's Son, but He also came to earth as a man. Have you let the power of that sink in, knowing Jesus truly understands the human emotions you experience?

The shortest verse in the Bible is, "Jesus wept" (John 11:35). Jesus wept when He found out His friend Lazarus had died. Some people say Jesus wept because He loved Lazarus so much. Others say it was because Jesus knew some of the people who gathered around would not believe He was the Messiah, even after Lazarus' resurrection. Still, others say Jesus wept because He saw the brokenness and grief of Mary, the sister of Lazarus, as she fell at His feet, and He grieved with her. Either way, we weep when a loved one dies or when our loved one isn't following Christ.

Consider how Jesus, the Messiah and King, was laughed at and mocked. Satan tempted and mocked Jesus in the desert for 40 days and nights. Many of the people in Jesus' hometown did not believe what Jesus taught. Many people mocked and laughed at Jesus as He hung on the cross.

Sometimes, people mock and laugh at us when we stand up for our beliefs or our faith, or when we step out to share God's love. Often when trials come, we pray they may pass us by—just like the prayer Jesus prayed in the Garden of Gethsemane. Ultimately, Jesus knew He was sent to earth to die, to set us free. In our trials, hopefully we, too, can say, "God, let Your will be done."

Do you ever feel God has forsaken you? There was a moment in Jesus' life when He felt abandoned by God. Because sin separates us from God, Jesus felt abandoned as He took on all the sins of the world, hanging on the cross. He came to earth to do God's will. He knew He was called, led, and empowered by God to sacrifice Himself to set us free from our sin. God promises to always be with us-it is our sin that separates us from Him, but Jesus made a way for us to have forgiveness.

Jesus also left us with a great example of loving one another. Jesus knew Judas would be the one to betray Him, yet He had no animosity toward Judas. Jesus still loved him—and that is the love we are called to have for one another.

Take time to reflect on Jesus' humanity and how He can relate to our emotions and feelings. He understands and wants us to know we can rely on God to help us on this journey.

Since the children have flesh and blood, he too shared in their humanity so that by his death he might destroy him who holds the power of death–that is, the devil.
~ Hebrews 2:14

Christine M. Fisher

75

Shattering the Darkness

She wrapped him in cloths and placed him in a manger,
because there was no room for them in the inn.
~ Luke 2:7

Thinking about the innkeeper who had no room available for Jesus is a good parallel of our own lives. Do we have "room" for Jesus in the "inn" of our heart? Have we accepted Jesus as Savior and Lord? Does He rule our lives? Or is the "inn" too busy with things that distract or take priority over living for Him?

The people walking in darkness have seen a great light;
on those living in the land of the shadow of death a light has dawned.
~ Isaiah 9:2

Jesus' birth, as well as the ultimate act of sacrificing His very life for us, *shattered the darkness*. Before God sent Jesus to earth, the people were in darkness from sin and evil. God's plan was to send the world a Savior, to save us from that evil. God did not want us to be in darkness.

Jesus entering the world means there is no more darkness, that *darkness is shattered* by the *light of Christ*. The darkness of *all* sin and evil is defeated. Jesus is the *light*. Our lives need to reflect His *light shattering the darkness*.

One Christmas, a group of us decided to go caroling to shut-ins. Each couple we visited was going through struggles and heartaches and was appreciative. The *light shattering the darkness* helped brighten their holidays. One family had a daughter going through a health trial. Her parents and I cried as we sang Christmas carols. Many of the carolers had prayed for her by name, not knowing the face. The couple showed them a picture so they could connect the face with the name.

Then, my eldest son had an idea to have *light shattering the darkness* for his grandmother who lives alone. He said, "We should make a meal for grandma and take it to her." This grandmother is a vegetarian, so my son came up with soup and dessert ideas. A few hours before arriving at grandma's house, I called to let her know when we would be there. Our entire family went to her apartment bringing the food. She was shocked to see us all. My husband brought his guitar and we sang a few Christmas carols. When we left, grandma was in tears—tears of happiness. I think the *light shattering the darkness* was a huge blessing to her. She will not soon forget that night. We have forged a new tradition to add to our holiday list.

Arise, shine, for your light has come, and the glory of the Lord rises upon you. See, darkness covers the earth and thick darkness is over the peoples, but the Lord rises upon you and his glory appears over you.
~ Isaiah 60:1-2

76

Carry My Cross

One Good Friday afforded me the opportunity to participate in something I had never done, *"A Witness Walk."* This involved walking in procession behind a 40-pound wooden cross carried by two people at a time. We walked through the streets, past houses and businesses, to commemorate Jesus' passion as He journeyed from Jerusalem to Calvary. This was the first time I was physically out on the streets proclaiming my faith and publicly displaying my love for the Lord. At first, it was a little intimidating, but I soon just concentrated on thinking of Jesus.

At intervals through the mile walk, we would pause, stand the cross up, listen to a reflection of Jesus' journey, pray and sing. The reflection reminded us of what Jesus went through and connected it with a current day equivalent. The leaders randomly selected people to take the megaphone and read the reflection.

The most humbling part of this journey was being asked to carry the wooden cross, not once, but three times. The first time I was at the back of the cross helping to carry it. I thought how special it would be to carry the cross in the front, on my shoulders, as I envisioned Jesus doing. A few stops later, God worked that out, and it was a very moving experience. When I carried the heavy cross, it was only five minutes, but it seemed as if the next stop would not come soon enough.

It was meaningful to experience physically what Jesus went through…for *my* sins, for *my* salvation, for *me* to live in eternity with Him. Jesus walked that lonely, hard road to Calvary where He faced death on that cross for *me,* and for *you.*

This Witness Walk was a good reminder of…

what Jesus endured for me.

how Jesus' life was about dying for other people a little each day.

ways I can die to myself.

how I can carry the cross for Jesus.

how I can be sensitive to the needs of others.

the importance of walking with others whose life intersects mine.

helping the poor, the needy, the person who is all alone.

Being asked to carry the cross, to walk in Jesus' footsteps, was an honor. It reminded me of Simon, the man who helped carry Jesus' cross. How often are we asked to carry the cross for a friend? How often do we, without being asked, see a need and walk alongside someone to help carry their cross? What ways can we challenge ourselves to help carry the cross for the people we encounter? It might be something as simple as sending a card to someone struggling to let them know we are praying for them. Perhaps it is a simple text letting someone know we will keep them in thought and prayer as they go through something.

Can someone say this about you? "Yes, I know I can always count on you to help carry my cross. Thank you."

A passerby named Simon, who was from Cyrene, was coming in from the countryside just then, and the soldiers forced him to carry Jesus' cross.
~ Mark 15:21 (NLT)

Christine M. Fisher

77

New Beginnings

New beginnings. When you hear these two words, what thoughts or feelings do they illicit? Feelings of happiness? Feelings of dread? I think it might depend on whether you are instigating the new beginning or whether someone or some event is responsible. Your response might also be related to whether you think it is a good beginning or a difficult beginning. What new beginnings have you experienced recently? Maybe…

starting a new school.

starting a new career.

starting a new church.

moving to a new state.

starting a new ministry.

starting a new life without a loved one.

starting a new team sport.

What would make your new beginnings a good experience? Maybe…

being welcomed with open arms.

knowing at least one person in your new adventure.

having confidence knowing you will do a great job.

knowing the Lord opened the doors for you.

knowing there are others supporting you in prayer.

knowing you are never alone; the Lord is always with you.

Think how Mary and His disciples and friends must have felt when Jesus died. They lost their son, teacher, and friend. They watched as He was tortured and hung on a tree. Can you relate to the sense of abandonment and helplessness they must have felt? They probably thought their lives could never go on. They had to face a new beginning, life without Jesus in their midst. Nevertheless, as time passed, they realized the terrible event of Jesus dying on the cross had a larger purpose.

**All who give their lives to Christ
can enjoy His daily presence on earth
and eternal life with Him in heaven.**

How did Jesus prepare for His new beginning?

He went alone to pray to God the Father.

He accepted what was to come.

He endured to set us free from our sin and bondage.

He walked the hills to Calvary carrying His heavy cross.

He endured suffering, was mocked and spat on.

When Jesus knew the final moment came, He said, "It is finished."

When we are faced with new beginnings, may we stop to think about Jesus' example to help us endure the changes. What can we learn from new beginnings?

It is good to grow and stretch.

The Lord is always there to guide us.

Despite being difficult, change can be a good thing.

New beginnings are not unique to people. When spring approaches each year, flowers bloom, the grass gets greener, and the birds return from the south. All creation experiences new beginnings.

*Forget the former things; do not dwell on the past. See, I am
doing a new thing. Now it springs up; do you not perceive it? I am
making a way in the desert and streams in the wasteland.*
~ Isaiah 43:18-19

Christine M. Fisher

78

Presence Not Presents

Christmas is a special time because we celebrate Christ's birth. God sent His only Son to earth, as a babe, to live like you and me, and to save us from our sin.

Each year my heart wants to capture the true meaning of Christmas rather than focusing on gift giving. Christmas is about being the voice and heart of Christ, through *presence* not presents. That is what makes my heart happy. I find joy in sharing with those less fortunate and reaching out to help others in whatever way possible. These thoughts were solidified for me the Christmas of 2011 when our area suffered a major flood. Many people lost a lot of their possessions and, even worse, their houses.

Our house is located on a slight hill, so we did not take on water. We had a few trees uprooted, and for four days, we were without electricity and running water. We are thankful we have a creek behind our house, so we were able to haul water into the house to flush the toilets. For two days, we had destruction and flooding of streets so we could only walk or bike (yes, my youngest son was crazy enough to try to bike through the water) to get out of the house. Trying to find passable roads was a challenge. The normal ten-minute drive took over an hour. That was the year we did not put up a Christmas tree. It did not seem "right" when so many people were left with nothing. Our family presents were kept simple, and we tried to help those who lost everything.

Christmas is about *presence*. Even today, we know people who are sick, confined to nursing homes or their homes, and others who are unemployed and seeking jobs to help keep their families afloat. With such hardship all around, it seems our voice and heart of being Christ for them, along with our *presence,* is the best thing we can offer. Singing carols and praying for people is always a blessing, which helps my heart feel the true meaning of Christmas. Bringing our *presence* more than presents is a joyous blessing.

And she gave birth to her firstborn son
and wrapped him in swaddling cloths
and laid him in a manger,
because there was no place
for them in the inn.
~ Luke 2:7 (ESV)

Christine M. Fisher

79

Our Road to Emmaus

The walk to Emmaus happened on the first day after Mary Magdalene and other women went to Jesus' tomb where they found the stone rolled away. The body of Jesus was gone. Two angels appeared to the women proclaiming Jesus was raised as He had foretold. The women ran to tell the apostles. Peter hurried to the tomb to see with his own eyes and was left wondering what happened to Jesus.

On the road to Emmaus were two apostles who were not part of Jesus' original twelve. We know one was named Cleopas, the other is unnamed. Visualize yourself as the "second" apostle walking with Cleopas to Emmaus (Luke 24:13-35).

As you and Cleopas walk from Jerusalem to the village of Emmaus, you discuss the events of the last few days. Jesus was put to death on the cross, Barabbas was set free, Jesus was in the tomb and now, three days later, His body has disappeared. Your faces are downcast as you try to figure things out. Suddenly, a man appears and walks with you. Neither of you recognize this person.

He wants to know what you are talking about. You tell him about Jesus of Nazareth, a prophet powerful in word and deed before God and all the people. How Jesus was sentenced to death, crucified and has now disappeared from the tomb where he lay. This person suddenly begins sharing with you, starting with Moses and all the prophets, explaining what the scriptures say concerning this Jesus. Your eyes and hearts do not recognize who is walking with you.

As the three of you approach the village of Emmaus, this third person acts as if he is going to be traveling further. You and Cleopas urge him strongly, "Stay with us, for it is nearly evening; the day is almost over." He agrees. As the three of you sit down for dinner, this third person takes bread, gives thanks, breaks it and shares it with you. It is then you and Cleopas realize who is in your midst–Jesus. As soon as you make the connection, Jesus disappears.

You turn to each other and ask, "Were not our hearts burning within us while he talked with us on the road and opened the scriptures to us?" You are excited to share the wonderful, good news that you have seen the risen Christ. You return immediately to Jerusalem and find the eleven and those assembled with them. The first words you and Cleopas hear from the eleven are, "It is true. The Lord has risen and has appeared to Simon." Cleopas and you agree and tell about your trip to Emmaus, and how you recognized Jesus when he broke the bread. You cannot contain your joy.

This story is so rich in content and applicable to our lives. Following are questions and thoughts to ponder:

> How many times do we fail to recognize Jesus' appearances in our lives?
>
> In what unexpected ways does Jesus enter our lives, walking with us?
>
> How often do we let our problems get the best of us, not recognizing Jesus is with us?
>
> Does doubt creep into our lives instead of believing the truth?
>
> Do we extend the invitation for Jesus to stay with us as we walk along the road with Him?
>
> Do we recognize Jesus in the breaking of the bread?
>
> Do our hearts burn within us when we open the scriptures?
>
> Do our hearts burn within us to share Jesus with others?
>
> Are our spiritual eyes open to see Jesus in each moment of our lives?

Christine M. Fisher

Do we share the Good News with our friends, family, and even strangers?

"It is true. The Lord has risen." Can we say and live out this truth?

Do we take time to recognize Jesus in every moment of our lives?

May you experience the road to Emmaus in your life, enabling you to make positive changes because of your journey with Jesus. May you, without any doubt, be able to say, "Yes, it is true, Jesus is risen. Stay with me, Lord. I know you will never leave me. Yes, Lord, I recognize your presence in my heart, in the scriptures, and in the breaking of the bread."

"Don't be alarmed," he said. "You are looking for
Jesus the Nazarene, who was crucified.
He has risen. He is not here. See the place where they laid him."
~ Mark 16:6

80

It's a Wonderful Life

One Christmas I attended a musical production of "*It's A Wonderful Life.*" The script came to life perfectly as each actor was well-cast. As I enjoyed the musical, there were two messages that jumped out.

In one scene, George Bailey tells Clarence, the angel, that he wishes he were never born. If you are familiar with the movie, you might recall the scenes show George what life on earth would be like without him. Any of the "great" things George did during his lifetime were suddenly not reflected in the lives of the people he knew and loved. Clarence says to George, "Strange isn't it? Each man's life touches so many other lives. When he isn't around, he leaves an awful hole, doesn't he?"[1]

Have you considered what other's lives would be like if you had never been born? Our lives and choices are so intertwined that one life affects many others. Your life is important no matter who you are or what you do.

Think for a few minutes what might be different if you had not been born:
> Maybe someone you led to Christ would not be living for Him now.
> Maybe someone you work with would not have had a chance to experience friendship at work.
> Maybe someone would not be alive today if you didn't rescue them from the tragic accident.
> Maybe that child in a foreign country would not have been able to go to school without your assistance.
> Maybe that sick person you prayed for would not have improved without your prayer.

Christine M. Fisher

Maybe that person you felt led to pray for, who was going to take their life, would not be alive today.

Think about that quote again. "Strange isn't it? Each man's life touches so many other lives. When he isn't around, he leaves an awful hole, doesn't he?" As we celebrate the birth of Jesus, doesn't that quote apply perfectly to Him? Jesus touches so many lives, ideally everybody's life—yours, mine, our neighbors, our relatives—all those we know and meet. When people do not know Jesus, there is an awful hole in their hearts they try to fill through other means–wealth, fame, relationships or power, to name a few. Only Jesus touches our lives and fills that awful hole.

The second message I took away was, yes, it really is a wonderful life. No matter what our life is like, no matter what we are going through, life is worth living. In the movie, George does not have much money and does not get to fulfill all his dreams. Eventually he realizes that love, family, and the townspeople are what are most valuable. George realizes, "It's a wonderful life."

A friend, despite difficult circumstances, is living out "It's a wonderful life" daily. She lives with a debilitating, chronic disease. Her mother recently had two major surgeries, and soon after, she learned her dad had cancer. Both parents were in the hospital one Thanksgiving Day. Despite the hardships, this friend continued to share inspiring thoughts testifying how her faith sustained her. She is living proof that, "It's a wonderful life."

We need to keep in mind how our life and actions influence every person we encounter. We can thank God for the influence Jesus has in filling the awful hole in our hearts. Remember, "It's a wonderful life."

You make known to me the path of life; in your
presence there is fullness of joy;
at your right hand are pleasures forevermore.
~ Psalm 16:11 (ESV)

81

Lord, is it I?

A friend mentioned a Maundy Thursday[2] program at his church. "Lord, is it I?" is the title of the living dramatization, written by Ernest K. Emurian, of Leonardo da Vinci's painting, "The Last Supper." Emurian wrote soliloquies[3] for each of the twelve apostles as they reflect on Jesus' words of "one of you will betray me" (John 13:21-27).

In the program, the twelve apostles each shared their stories of when they first met Jesus, their experiences with Him, and their personal thoughts and feelings about Jesus. Each had their own viewpoint of the different events. After they shared these reflections, each apostle looked to Jesus and asked, "Lord, is it I?"

> Jesus dipped the bread and handed it to Judas, the one Jesus knew would betray Him that evening. Judas betrayed Jesus with a kiss (Matthew 26:47-49).

> Peter denied knowing Jesus three times before the cock crowed, just as Jesus foretold. Simon Peter betrayed Jesus by his denial (Luke 22:59-61).

My eyes were opened to another way Simon Peter betrayed Jesus. Simon Peter betrayed Jesus by trying to thwart God's plan.

> *Then Simon Peter, who had a sword, drew it*
> *and struck the high priest's servant,*
> *cutting off his right ear. (The servant's name was*
> *Malchus.) Jesus commanded Peter,*

Christine M. Fisher

"Put your sword away.
Shall I not drink the cup the Father has given me?"
~ John 18:10-11

The apostle Thomas was present at the Last Supper. After Jesus died, He appeared to all the disciples except for Thomas. Thomas betrayed Jesus by doubting Him unless he could see proof (John 20:24-25).

Even though Jesus knew Judas would betray Him with a kiss, and Simon Peter would deny knowing Him, and Thomas would need to see to believe, Jesus loved them dearly. He felt no ill will against them. Jesus extended the invitation to spend His last meal with them.

How appropriate that we can apply this thought of betraying Jesus to our own lives asking this same question, "Lord, is it I?" Lord, how many times do we betray you?

Take a few moments to reflect on that question. What are ways we betray Jesus?

> We do not spend time in prayer daily.
> We do not share with others what our relationship with Jesus means.
> We deny His power working through us.
> We do not share our time, talent, and treasure.
> We doubt Jesus' presence in our lives.
> We doubt the power of the resurrection that lives in us.

Does Jesus still love us unconditionally even when we betray Him? Yes, His love is unconditional. Consider how Simon Peter responded after he realized he did indeed deny knowing Jesus.

And he went outside and wept bitterly.
~ Luke 22:62

He felt remorse. We learn he continued to love and serve others in Jesus' name. After Jesus' death and resurrection, one of the times He appeared to His apostles, there was a conversation between Jesus and Simon Peter.

When they had finished eating, Jesus said to Simon Peter, "Simon son of John, do you love me more than these?" "Yes, Lord," he said, "you know that I love you." Jesus said, "Feed my lambs." Again Jesus said, "Simon son of John, do you love me?" He answered, "Yes, Lord, you know that I love you." Jesus said, "Take care of my sheep." The third time he said to him, "Simon son of John, do you love me?" Peter was hurt because Jesus asked him the third time, "Do you love me?" He said, "Lord, you know all things; you know that I love you." Jesus said, "Feed my sheep. Very truly I tell you, when you were younger you dressed yourself and went where you wanted; but when you are old you will stretch out your hands, and someone else will dress you and lead you where you do not want to go." Jesus said this to indicate the kind of death by which Peter would glorify God. Then he said to him, "Follow me."
~ John 21:15-19

What a significant parallel that Jesus asked Peter three times if he loved Him. Jesus forgave Simon Peter for betraying Him, and Simon Peter continued to further Jesus' kingdom on earth. What great encouragement. What can we do when we realize we have betrayed Jesus? Repent from our heart, ask Jesus to help us, confess our sins, and seek His forgiveness.

Consequently, you are no longer foreigners and strangers, but fellow citizens with God's people and also members of his household, built on the foundation of the apostles and prophets, with Christ Jesus himself as the chief cornerstone. In him the whole building is joined together and rises to become a holy temple in the Lord.
~ Ephesians 2:19-21

Christine M. Fisher

82

Resurrection Power

The most important part of our faith is the resurrection of Jesus. Consider the power there is in Jesus' resurrection when we say, "He is risen. Alleluia!"

Let's step back and look at some amazing miracles that happened when Jesus died. There was great power in Jesus' death as well as His resurrection.

> *And when Jesus had cried out again in a loud voice, he gave up his Spirit. At that moment the curtain of the temple was torn in two from top to bottom. The earth shook and the rocks split. The tombs broke open and the bodies of many holy people who had died were raised to life. They came out of the tombs, and after Jesus' resurrection they went into the holy city and appeared to many people.*
> ~ Matthew 27:50-53

From the Old Testament, we know the temple had a curtain between the Holy Place and the Most Holy Place. The Most Holy Place is where the Ark of the Testimony was placed. It represented God's throne room. Once a year, only the High Priest was permitted to enter the Most Holy Place to enter God's presence and seek atonement for Israel's sins.

> *Hang the inner curtain from clasps, and put the Ark of the Covenant in the room behind it. This curtain will separate the Holy Place from the Most Holy Place.*
> ~ Exodus 26:33 (NLT)

*"Aaron shall make atonement on its horns once a year. With the blood
of the sin offering of atonement he shall make atonement for it once in
the year throughout your generations. It is most holy to the Lord."*
~ Exodus 30:10 (ESV)

When Jesus died, the curtain of the temple was torn in two, from top to
bottom. This signified that Jesus made it possible for all believers, even the
Gentiles, to enter God's presence at any time.

*But when Christ appeared as a high priest of the good things to come,
he entered through the greater and more perfect tabernacle, not made
with hands, that is to say, not of this creation; and not through the
blood of goats and calves, but through his own blood, He entered
the holy place once for all, having obtained eternal redemption.*
~ Hebrews 9:11-12 (NASB)

Can you image the earth shaking and rocks splitting right before your
eyes? Tombs of the saints broke open with their bodies being raised to life.
What an incredible miracle. These same people appeared to others after
Jesus' resurrection.

Fast forward three days.

*The angel said to the women, "Do not be afraid, for I know that
you are looking for Jesus, who was crucified. He is not here; he has
risen, just as he said. Come and see the place where he lay.
Then go quickly and tell his disciples: "He has risen
from the dead and is going ahead of you into Galilee.
There you will see him. Now I have told you."*
~ Matthew 28:5-7

Consider the power in Jesus' resurrection when we say, "He is risen.
Alleluia!" Jesus' resurrection is not just a one-time historical event we

Christine M. Fisher

celebrate each year. The same power that raised Jesus from the dead is available in our lives, every day.

How?

> God forgives our sins because Jesus paid the price for our sins.
> We no longer need to offer Him sacrifices.
> We will never see death since we will spend eternity with God in heaven.
> We can love others unconditionally like God loves us.
> Even through the struggles of life, we are assured God works everything out for our good.
> Suffering is a part of life, and we know God is always with us.
> We can "die" to ourselves, knowing Jesus did the same for us. We can replace fear with faith.
> The fruits of the Spirit are a part of our life: love, joy, peace, patience, kindness, goodness, faithfulness, gentleness and self-control.

I want to know Christ and the power of his resurrection and the fellowship of sharing in his sufferings, becoming like him in his death, and so, somehow, to attain to the resurrection from the dead.
~ Philippians 3:10-11

83

Christmas Every Day

"And peace on earth will come to stay, when we live Christmas every day."
~ Helen Steiner Rice

A Christmas card I received posed this question: "How can we live Christmas every day? Why can't we be filled with joy, unselfish giving, peace, and love toward others?"

Why should we unselfishly give? To find true joy and peace of mind. Unselfish giving does not even require money making it even cheaper than buying actual Christmas presents. What can we give unselfishly to others?

Time to listen with our heart.

Helping the maid at a hotel by putting our linens in a pile.

Visiting a shut-in who is lonely.

Typing a quick message to tell a friend we are thinking of them.

Being patient with the driver who merged into our lane without signaling.

A heart of compassion for someone who is suffering.

A sincere compliment about someone's character.

An encouraging word.

Offering to help someone carry a heavy load.

Taking a coworker to the store if they don't have transportation.

Can we find one way to unselfishly give to others every day?

What a blessing true joy and peace of mind are. It is a great gift to know we did our part to help live Christmas every day.

My command is this: love each other as I have loved you.
~ John 15:12

Christine M. Fisher

84

My Peace I Give You

One Easter season, I read about Jesus' last days, His death and resurrection, from the perspective of all four gospels to see the differences and the similarities. I continued reading into the book of Acts as I journeyed with the disciples after Jesus ascended into heaven. Peace is a recurring theme that struck me, especially in the gospel of John. Jesus wanted His disciples to have peace, both when He died and after He returned to heaven. Along with His peace, Jesus also commissioned the disciples, telling them what they needed to do after His return to His Father.

Since we participate in these same celebrations each liturgical year, we should know Jesus imparts these same gifts to us. Our lives should model those of the first disciples since we, too, are called to be His disciples.

There were three occasions where Jesus comforted His disciples before He was arrested. The setting for this first instance was after Jesus told His disciples He would only be with them a little longer.

> *"Do not let your hearts be troubled. Trust in God; trust also in me. In my Father's house are many rooms; if it were not so, I would have told you. I am going there to prepare a place for you. And if I go and prepare a place for you, I will come back and take you to be with me that you also may be where I am. You know the way to the place where I am going."*
> ~ John 14:1-4

Isn't it endearing to hear Jesus' concern for us? He does not want our heart to be troubled. Jesus knows the antidote for our troubled heart is trust. Everything is going to be okay; God's plan is always at work.

The second instance was when Jesus assured the disciples, He would never leave them orphaned. The Father would send the Holy Spirit who would remind them of everything Jesus shared. Again, Jesus said,

> *"Peace I leave with you; my peace I give you. I*
> *do not give to you as the world gives.*
> *Do not let your hearts be troubled and do not be afraid."*
> ~ John 14:27

When we are in total fellowship with God, we have true peace, the peace the world cannot understand. It is a peace that surpasses all understanding, a real and present peace deep within our heart. Truly Jesus wants us to know our heart does not need to be troubled or afraid any longer.

The disciples were confused when Jesus told them,

> *"Soon you will not see me, but later you will see me*
> *again since I am returning to the Father."*
> ~ John 16:17

Jesus then said,

> *"I have told you these things, so that in me you may have peace.*
> *In this world you will have trouble. But take*
> *heart. I have overcome the world."*
> ~ John 16:33

Jesus shared, for a third time, despite the troubles we face in this world, we can replace them with His peace. He will gain victory over this world.

After the death of Jesus, he was laid in a tomb. The best news, the Good News, is that three days later He rose from the dead. From Matthew's gospel, we learn that Mary Magdalene and the other Mary found the tomb empty and did not know where Jesus was. The women hurried away,

"afraid yet filled with joy."
~ Matthew 28:8

As they went to share the news with the disciples, Jesus met them and said,

"Do not be afraid."
~ Matthew 28:10

Jesus' first risen appearance was to these women. He wanted to make sure they were not afraid.

From John's gospel, we find three more cases where Jesus, in His risen body, extends His peace to us. On the evening of the first day of the week, when the eleven were together behind locked doors for fear of the Jews, Jesus appeared and said,

"Peace be with you."
~ John 20:19

The disciples observed the scars in His hands and side, and again Jesus said,

"Peace be with you. As the Father has sent me, I am sending you."
~ John 20:21

Jesus then breathed on the ten disciples and said,

"Receive the Holy Spirit. If you forgive anyone his sins, they are forgiven; if you do not forgive them, they are not forgiven."
~ John 20:22-23

The risen Jesus extended His peace to the disciples, wanting them to know everything was being fulfilled according to God's plan. Jesus prepared them for the arrival of the Holy Spirit so they would never be alone. The Spirit would guide them. Jesus gave them power to forgive sins encouraging them to forgive others so their sins would be forgiven too.

Jesus wanted to make sure all His disciples experienced the peace of knowing the risen Jesus. He appeared once more to His disciples, along the Sea of Galilee. This is where Jesus forgave and redeemed Peter for his denial, extending His unconditional love. Peter was forgiven just as we are when we repent of our sins. Soak up Jesus' great love and forgiveness. He wants us to follow Him.

The Great Commission from Jesus to the eleven disciples says,

"Therefore go and make disciples of all nations, baptizing them
in the name of the Father and of the Son and of the Holy Spirit,
and teaching them to obey everything I have commanded you.
And surely I am with you always, to the very end of the age."
~ Matthew 28:19-20

Reflecting on Jesus' last encounters with His disciples, the peace He imparted, and the instructions of His Great Commission, think about how they experienced this perfect sequence of events:

"The presence of God gives you
the peace of God which leads to
the power of God which enables
the people of God to carry out
the plans of God."

What a perfect summary. A pastor friend gets credit for the wisdom and truth of that ending sequence.

My prayer is that each day you will experience the presence of God giving you the peace of God, which He extends to you, leading you to the power of God which enables you, the people of God, to carry out the plans of God.

You will keep in perfect peace all who trust in you,
all whose thoughts are fixed on you.
~ Isaiah 26:3 (NLT)

85

Jesus Meets Us

"The Holy Spirit has different signs for each of us." It was a simple sentence from a friend that resonated with me, especially after hearing a sermon two days later. Yes, I believe the Holy Spirit has different signs for each of us, speaking to us in different ways, in ways we are individually best able to hear Him. Fast forward to this scripture passage I heard after my friend's comment:

> *On the evening of that first day of the week, when the disciples*
> *were together, with the doors locked for fear of the Jewish leaders,*
> *Jesus came and stood among them and said, "Peace be with you."*
> *After he said this, he showed them his hands and side. The disciples*
> *were overjoyed when they saw the Lord. Again, Jesus said, "Peace*
> *be with you. As the Father has sent me, I am sending you."*
> ~ John 20:19-21

Despite the doors being locked, Jesus appeared in the midst of the disciples. The disciples were fearful and anxious, hiding from the Jews, because Jesus was crucified. They did not know what the Jews would do next...maybe even kill them. Jesus knew what they were experiencing and met them in their need. Jesus came to assure them everything would be fine and to bring them His peace; to let them know everything would be all right.

Think about a time when the Lord stepped in and said to you, "Peace be with you. Everything is going to be okay."

And with that he breathed on them and said, "Receive the
Holy Spirit. If you forgive anyone's sins, their sins are forgiven;
if you do not forgive them, they are not forgiven."
~ John 20:22-23

Did you notice how Jesus breathed on the disciples and then they received the Holy Spirit, the third person of the Trinity? Think back to Genesis when God formed man.

He breathed into his nostrils the breath of life;
and man became a living soul.
~ Genesis 2:7 (KJV)

With that first breath God brought man to life; now Jesus breathed on the disciples and brought the Holy Spirit alive in them. Can you think of a time when you felt Jesus breathe the Holy Spirit into your life?

We also see how Jesus met Thomas where he was.

Now Thomas (also known as Didymus), one of the Twelve, was not with
the disciples when Jesus came. So the other disciples told him, "We have
seen the Lord." But he said to them, "Unless I see the mark of the nails in
his hands and put my finger where the nails were, and put my hand into
his side, I will not believe." A week later his disciples were in the house
again and Thomas was with them. Though the doors were locked, Jesus
came and stood among them and said, "Peace be with you." Then he said
to Thomas, "Put your finger here; see my hands. Reach out your hand and
put it into my side. Stop doubting and believe." Thomas said to him, "My
Lord and my God." Then Jesus told him, "Because you have seen me, you
have believed; blessed are those who have not seen and yet have believed."
~ John 20:24-29

Thomas was not with the other disciples when Jesus appeared to them a week earlier, so Thomas did not believe Jesus was alive. What did Jesus do?

He waited a week and then appeared again, even though the doors were locked. The first thing Jesus did was speak directly to Thomas, offering him peace. Before Thomas could say anything, Jesus told him, *"put your finger here and see my hands..."* Jesus knew what Thomas said to the other disciples about his unbelief and so Jesus met Thomas right where he was. He knew Thomas needed to see and put his fingers in the nail wounds to believe. Can you think of a time when you needed tangible evidence to feel His presence in your life?

Jesus performed many other signs in the presence of his disciples,
which are not recorded in this book. But these are written
that you may believe that Jesus is the Christ, the Son of God,
and that by believing you may have life in his name.
~ John 20:30-31

Jesus met the disciples where they were, providing signs to reveal who He was to help them believe. John tells us that Jesus meets us right where we are, providing us with the words and knowledge of what we need, when we need it. How blessed the disciples were to be in Jesus' presence. And how blessed we are to have the words He left us—for our sustenance, benefit, and growth.

Declare his glory among the nations, his marvelous deeds among all peoples.
~ Psalm 96:3

86

Humility

One Christmas season I thought about the humility surrounding Christ's entrance into this world. The definition of humility is the feeling or attitude that you have no special importance that makes you better than others; a lack of pride.

Consider Mary, the mother of Jesus as someone who exemplifies humility. We do not hear of her being popular in this world or of high status. Here she was just a young woman,

> *...a virgin pledged to be married to a man*
> *named Joseph, a descendant of David.*
> *The angel, Gabriel told Mary, "The Holy Spirit will come on*
> *you, and the power of the Most High will overshadow you. So*
> *the holy one to be born will be called the Son of God."*
> *"I am the Lord's servant," Mary answered. "May your*
> *word to me be fulfilled." Then the angel left her.*
> ~Luke 1:27, 35, 38

Her response displays humility. She was trusting God and ready to be a part of His plan. She graciously accepted God's plan of being the mother of Jesus. Mary was the humble maidservant of God who, through the Holy Spirit, birthed our Savior.

Just as important is to keep in mind the humility of Joseph. Upon first hearing that Mary was going to have a child, Joseph thought about divorcing her, but...

...an angel of the Lord appeared to him in a dream and said,
"Joseph son of David, do not be afraid to take Mary home as
your wife, because what is conceived in her is from the Holy
Spirit. She will give birth to a son, and you are to give him the
name Jesus, because he will save his people from their sins."
~ Matthew 1:20-21

Joseph did what the angel commanded. Taking Mary for his wife, when she was pregnant with the Son of God, was humility. He, too, gives a powerful example of doing God's will.

Despite being the Savior of the world, Jesus was certainly born in humility. He was born while his parents journeyed, on foot, to their hometown after registering for a census.

While they were there, the time came for the baby to be born,
and she gave birth to her firstborn, a son. She wrapped
him in cloths and placed him in a manger,
because there was no guest room available for them.
~ Luke 2:6-7

Imagine giving birth to the Savior of the world in a barn and having to place the baby in an animal trough. Jesus was born in the humblest of ways, yet He is the Savior of the world.

Ponder the powerful example of humility that Mary, Joseph, and Jesus gave us over 2,000 years ago. Let us lead lives of humility, following the example of Jesus.

God opposes the proud but gives grace to the humble. Humble yourselves,
therefore, under God's mighty hand, that he may lift you up in due time.
~ 1 Peter 5:5-6

87

Victory

We have *victory* through Jesus' death on the cross. From the Old Testament we read:

They (the Israelites) traveled from Mount Hor along the route to the Red Sea, to go around Edom. But the people grew impatient on the way; they spoke against God and against Moses, and said "Why have you brought us up out of Egypt to die in the desert? There is no bread! There is no water! And we detest this miserable food!" Then the Lord sent venomous snakes among them; they bit the people and many Israelites died. The people came to Moses and said, "We sinned when we spoke against the Lord and against you. Pray that the Lord will take the snakes away from us." So Moses prayed for the people. The Lord said to Moses, "Make a snake and put it up on a pole; anyone who is bitten can look at it and live." So Moses made a bronze snake and put it up on a pole. Then when anyone was bitten by a snake and looked at the bronze snake, he lived.
~ Numbers 21:4-9

Fast forward to the New Testament where we read about Jesus being sent to earth by God, His Father. Jesus knew God's plan from the beginning and shared that message in the following passages:

And as Moses lifted up the bronze snake on a pole in the wilderness,
so the Son of Man must be lifted up,
so that everyone who believes in him will have eternal life.
~ John 3:14-15 (NLT)

Christine M. Fisher

So Jesus said, "When you have lifted up the Son of Man on the cross,
then you will understand that I Am he. I do nothing on my own
but say only what the Father taught me."
~ John 8:28 (NLT)

The time for judging this world has come, when Satan,
the ruler of this world, will be cast out.
And when I am lifted up from the earth, I will draw everyone to myself.
~ John 12:31-32 (NLT)

Think back to our first parents, Adam and Eve, when they were in the Garden of Eden. What "tricked" them into eating from the fruit of the tree that God specifically told them not to eat? A serpent. What did Adam and Eve eat? The fruit from the *tree* of the knowledge of good and evil.

How ironic, years later, God told Moses to make a bronze serpent and to put it on a cross; a cross which was made from a *tree*. If the Israelites who were bitten by a snake then looked at the serpent on the cross, they would be healed. The very thing, a serpent, that caused humankind to sever its pure, unadulterated relationship with God was now healing the people who looked at the serpent on the cross. What did Jesus die upon? A cross, made from a *tree*. No longer was there a serpent upon the cross; but Jesus.

What a powerful, symbolic plan for God to send His only Son, Jesus, to physically hang on the cross, to show how the cross is the triumph, the *victory* that is ours through Jesus. Through God's great power and wisdom, the cross transformed suffering into redemption. Jesus, our Savior, saved us from our sins; even from the very first sin in the garden. Jesus on the cross is the ultimate victory over the serpent, the fall, and sin. The cross of Jesus is to be lifted. When we lift Jesus on the cross, we see Him and are drawn to Him. How symbolic Jesus provides that victory over the serpent who sought to rule this world. The *victory* is in Jesus on the cross. The ultimate VICTORY over death. 221

How is the cross a victory?

> It gives humanity a Savior who restored the broken relationship caused by Adam and Eve.
>
> Instead of being condemned to death for our sinful nature, we are set free.
>
> We are released from bondage of the Law; replaced with the law of love.
>
> It is a perfect example of Jesus' obedience to God, His Father.

Why is victory needed?

> To restore our right relationship with God, our Father, so we can spend eternity together.

How do we experience this victory on earth?

> In a personal relationship with God.
>
> In forgiveness of our sins.
>
> In God's mercy and grace.
>
> In God's unconditional love.
>
> In sharing God's love with all we encounter.
>
> In choosing obedience to God.
>
> With living in hope.

How do we experience this victory eternally?

> We have the assurance of living with God in the heavenly kingdom for all eternity; in a place where there is only light and goodness.

How fitting that Adam and Eve ate from a tree to cause our fall, and *Jesus hung on a tree to redeem us from the fall.* May we be reminded that the crosses we bear and the sufferings we endure are just a small sharing in the redemption of Jesus' cross. Think of how Jesus' arms were outstretched on that cross, arms ready to embrace us with His great love.

The story does not end with Jesus dying on the cross. Three days later He was resurrected and ascended into heaven to be reunited with God. *Victory is ours* through Jesus and the cross. Eternal life is ours.

Celebrate the *victory* on the cross that He endured for your salvation. Take a few minutes to gaze upon a crucifix and reflect on Jesus' great love for *you*. Realize if you were the *only* person ever, Jesus would have died on the cross for *you*. Celebrate the *victory* that is yours.

For the message of the cross is foolishness to those who are perishing,
but to us who are being saved it is the power of God.
~ 1 Corinthians 1:18

88

Encouragement

God has given us all gifts to help build His kingdom; ways to glorify Him in our everyday lives.

> *We have different gifts, according to the grace given us. If a man's gift is prophesying, let him use it in proportion of his faith. If it is serving, let him serve; if it is teaching, let him teach; if it is encouraging, let him encourage; if it is contributing to the needs of others, let him give generously; if it is leadership, let him govern diligently; if it is showing mercy, let him do it cheerfully.*
> ~ Romans 12:6-8

The word "gifts" in this passage translates from Greek to the word charismata, "referring to special gifts of grace—freely given by God to His people to meet the needs of the body of Christ."[4] We are all given gifts of grace to meet the needs of the body, to build up God's kingdom. We are accountable for how well we use these gifts for His glory. The Romans passage above mentions the gifts of teaching, encouraging, sharing and leading.

The two gifts that best describe me are serving and encouraging. I was pleasantly surprised one day to find a Biblical person who modeled the gift of encouragement. It was Barnabas, whose name means "Son of encouragement." It is said of Barnabas that "he sought out others and assisted them in whatever way he could, thus being an encourager."

What are some ways we can be an encourager—inspiring with courage, spirit, or confidence—in others' lives?

Letting others know we are praying for them, even our pastor, deacon, or music minister.

Sending a heartfelt note to someone who has had a great influence in our life.

Taking time to phone someone to let them know we are thinking of them; staying connected in friendship.

Sharing how someone touched our life in a positive way.

Pointing out how we see God in others' actions.

Boosting someone's self-esteem.

Praying for those in need—friends, acquaintances, or strangers.

Sharing God's word to uplift someone.

Sending a card to a shut-in.

Pointing out moments we see God in our life.

Something I never considered is how the Holy Spirit is the greatest encourager we have. He is God's presence on earth. Jesus speaks to His disciples, and ultimately to us, to comfort them through understanding the Holy Spirit.

> *But when the Helper comes, whom I will send to*
> *you from the Father, the Spirit of truth,*
> *who proceeds from the Father, he will bear witness about me.*
> *And you also will bear witness, because you have*
> *been with me from the beginning.*
> ~ John 15:26-27 (ESV)

> *Nevertheless, I tell you the truth: it is to your advantage*
> *that I go away, for if I do not go away, the Helper will not*
> *come to you. But if I go, I will send him to you.*
> ~ John 16:7 (ESV)

The word "helper" comes from the Greek word "parakletos," which literally translates to "one called to the side of another." What a perfect definition of the Spirit. We should take great comfort that Jesus sent us the Holy Spirit, the Encourager, to walk with us on life's journey. He did not leave us orphans to fend for ourselves.

What are some ways, the Helper, the Encourager, walks beside us daily? He is...

>that still, quiet voice that leads us to action.
>the one who gives us the confirmations of things we should do.
>the peace that comes when we know the path we should take.
>the strength we receive when we take on a new ministry we thought we could not do.
>the boldness to step out of the boat with Jesus.
>the one who gives us the words to share Christ with someone who doesn't know Him.
>the one who opens the eyes of our hearts and minds to new insights when reading scripture.

The Holy Spirit is the ultimate encourager, enabling us to be more Christ-like. Encouragers are people who....

>see what can be done.
>see how God works through us all.
>see possibilities.
>find ways to support others.
>pray for others.
>build others up to grow in their faith.
>bring hope to a dark world.
>have a lasting effect on others' lives.

We can all practice spreading encouragement—inspiring courage, spirit, and confidence—to at least one person every day. Help spread the goodness of the Holy Spirit. You, too, can step out in faith and be an encourager.

Christine M. Fisher

Then the church throughout Judea, Galilee and Samaria enjoyed a time of peace. It was strengthened and encouraged by the Holy Spirit, it grew in numbers, living in the fear of the Lord.

~ Acts 9:31

89

Building the Kingdom—
Unlikely People

Jesus uses the most unlikely people to build His kingdom on earth.

Do you ever think you are not important in the kingdom of God?
Do you ever think you have done so many "bad" things God cannot love you?
Do you ever think you are so messed up God cannot possibly use you for furthering His kingdom on earth?
Do you ever think God cannot possibly use you for a purpose in His kingdom?
Do you ever think you have failed God and are not worthy?

Well, I have some encouragement for you. I will say it again.
Jesus uses the most unlikely people to build His kingdom on earth.

One biblical person that exemplifies this is Simon Peter. What do we know about Peter?

Jesus had big plans for Peter from the beginning, foreshadowed by the name Jesus gave him, Cephas, which in Aramaic translates to "rock" (John 1:35-42).
Peter was a simple fisherman (Matthew 4:18-20).
Peter felt unworthy and sinful in Jesus' presence (Luke 5:1-10).
Peter did not want Jesus to wash his feet because of his humility and pride (John 13:1-17).
Peter denied knowing Jesus three times (Luke 22:54-62).
Peter walked on water but began to sink when he started to doubt (Matthew 14:22-33).

Peter declared, "Jesus is the Messiah." Jesus called Peter to be the *rock* of the church (Matthew 16:13-20).

Jesus forgave Peter and commissioned his kingdom purpose (John 21:15-17).

Have you stopped to reflect on the *why* of Peter denying Jesus, not once but three times?

Falling into temptation got the best of him.

His body was tired, so it was harder to keep spiritually alive.

He had a hard time praying.

He was hanging with the "wrong" crowd.

He let fear of what others thought overtake him.

He was afraid he might be put to death like Jesus.

To fulfill Jesus' prophecy.

I cannot help but be in awe of how Peter *repented* of his denial of Christ. I wonder if it was because...

Jesus turned and looked directly into Peter's eyes.

he knew how much Jesus loved him.

he knew Jesus was indeed the Messiah.

he spent three years seeing the miracles and healings Jesus provided for others.

he knew the depth of Jesus' love for every person he encountered.

he saw firsthand how Jesus forgave everyone who confessed their sins.

he wanted to spend eternity with Jesus in heaven.

Isn't it inspiring to see how Jesus used Peter, just an ordinary person, to ultimately be the *rock* upon which Jesus' church continued?

Do you see yourself in Peter?

Do you sometimes "deny" Christ for some of the same reasons Peter did?

Are you quick to repent when you fall into sin and temptation?

Do you know the depth of Jesus' great love for you?

How did Jesus use Peter to build His kingdom on earth? Peter was a simple fisherman, but Jesus used him to be a fisher of men. In the early days, Peter was anything but a rock, but by God's grace, Peter became Cephas. Jesus knew His plan for Simon Peter to become a *rock* when He first encountered him. Peter found courage in Christ when stepping out of the boat.

Peter denied knowing Christ, yet repented and ultimately loved Christ above all else. Peter was commissioned to carry on the church…
> to feed the lambs, (possibly the laity of the church).
> to take care of Jesus' sheep, (possibly the church leaders).
> to feed Jesus' sheep, (possibly the church congregation).

Peter was the one who shared the gospel, the Good News, at the first Pentecost. Peter was the leader of the church in Jerusalem, the first center of the church. Peter wrote two epistles, 1 Peter and 2 Peter. These were written as instructional letters for the early church. Tradition tells us that Peter was crucified upside down, as he did not feel worthy to die on the cross the same way Jesus did.

Just as Jesus did in Peter's life, so Jesus does in our lives…
> He molds us to be the people He intends us to be, if we are willing.
> He uses our imperfection, failures, and shortcomings and makes something beautiful of us.
> as imperfect as we are, Jesus can use each one of us if we love Him with our whole heart and yield to Him.

Yes, *Jesus uses the most unlikely people to build His kingdom on earth. You* are an important part of that kingdom.

> *But seek first his kingdom and his righteousness, and*
> *all these things will be given to you as well.*
> ~ Matthew 6:33

90

Peace

One of the greatest gifts Jesus left us is the gift of peace. Peace that can bring us joy and comfort despite our circumstances. His peace is made available to us as we continually seek Him. To possess His peace makes all the difference in our lives.

When Jesus, in His resurrected state, visited the disciples, He greeted them by saying, "Peace."

> *On the evening of that first day of the week, when the disciples*
> *were together, with the doors locked for fear of the Jews, Jesus*
> *came and stood among them and said, "Peace be with you."*
> ~ John 20:19

> *Again Jesus said, "Peace be with you. As the*
> *Father has sent me, I am sending you."*
> ~ John 20:21

> *A week later his disciples were in the house again, and Thomas*
> *was with them. Though the doors were locked, Jesus came*
> *and stood among them and said, "Peace be with you."*
> ~ John 20:26

In these verses, Jesus was preparing His disciples to experience true peace when He sent the Holy Spirit after He ascended into Heaven.

> *"All this I have spoken while still with you. But the Counselor, the*
> *Holy Spirit, whom the Father will send in my name, will teach you*
> *all things and will remind you of everything I have said to you.*

Peace I leave with you; my peace I give you. I
do not give to you as the world gives.
Do not let your hearts be troubled and do not be afraid."
~ John 14:25-27

The peace we possess should not be based on our circumstances or what others think of us. We all have troubles, but God's peace is triumphant over all. Therefore, the next time you have a day or week where everything seems to go wrong...

the kids are sick,

you have a flat tire at the most inopportune time,

you oversleep and are late for work,

you find out you have some disease,

... dig down deep and cling to the peace only God can provide. The peace that surpasses all understanding. It is His peace that sustains us even during the troubled, hard times as long as we cling to Him and trust in His ways.

Do you ever feel God's peace in the beautiful world He created for us...

in a beautiful sunset or rainbow that just takes your breath away?

in the sun rising slowly over the peaceful waters of the ocean?

These things we behold with our eyes remind us of the peace God offers. Try each day to tap into the wonderful power of His peace.

And the peace of God, which transcends all understanding,
will guard your hearts and your minds in Christ Jesus.
~ Philippians 4:7

CONCLUSION

Thank you for taking time to travel and explore life through the lens of my heart. I hope you can relate to events that have occurred in your life through reading the experiences I shared. God made each of us unique in our own ways, yet we all have threads of similarities running through our lives.

May your faith journey be inspired with hope and light in seeing how the Lord is working in your life; even in the simplest of moments. Truly, God's presence is illuminated in all creation, in scripture, in every person we meet, and in Jesus. May this be the beginning of a deeper journey with God, with His presence illuminating your daily walk more and more.

ABOUT THE AUTHOR

Christine Fisher defines herself in this way, "I am a simple, ordinary gal, a child of God, a lover of Jesus, a daughter, wife and mother. I am also an introvert who enjoys sharing God-stories through writing and in small intimate settings."

Christine models her life after the ministry of Jesus. She serves others in little things, like Christmas caroling to shut-ins, holding the tiniest of babies in the NICU, giving rides to those without transportation, serving in the soup kitchen, holding the hands of friends, and praying over strangers. She finds joy in being an encourager by sending cards, praying, visiting, and providing affirming words.

Through the written word, Christine shares what is in her heart about Jesus, hoping to inspire and encourage others in their faith journey. She has the "eyes of God," and sees His presence, goodness, and grace through the ordinary things in life, whether it be a seashell on the beach or a boulder on the mountaintop. Being able to express her thoughts in writing and through the spoken word has helped her deepen her faith and grow closer in her relationship with Jesus.

Christine and her husband, Mark, live in upstate New York. They are the parents of three adult children. She enjoys spending quiet time in nature worshiping the Creator.

Publish his glorious deeds among the nations.
Tell everyone about the amazing things he does.
~ 1 Chronicles 16:24 (NLT)

I am the vine; you are the branches. If you remain in me and I in you,
you will bear much fruit; apart from me you can do nothing!
~ John 15:5

Commit to the Lord whatever you do, and he will establish your plans.
~ Proverbs 16:3

As the rain and the snow come down from heaven, and do not
return to it without watering the earth and making it bud and
flourish, so that it yields seed for the sower and bread for the eater,
so is my word that goes out from my mouth: It will not return to me
empty but will accomplish what I desire and achieve the purpose for
which I sent it. You will go out in joy and be led forth in peace.
~ Isaiah 55:10

You can receive Christine's weekly posts by subscribing at www.hopetoinspireyou.com or by following her on Facebook at *hopetoinspireyou*.

NOTES

[1] *It's a Wonderful Life.* Directed by Frank Capra, performance by James Stewart, Donna Reed, Lionel Barrymore, and Thomas Mitchell, RKO, 1946.

[2] Maundy Thursday is the Thursday before Easter. Christians believe this to be the day when Jesus celebrated the Last Supper with His disciples (his final Passover meal). It is also when Jesus washed the feet of His disciples in a display of servanthood and humility. He told His disciples to do the same for one another.

[3] Soliloquies for the Twelve Apostles. Published in "More Plays and Pageants for Many Occasions," written by Ernest K. Emurian. Published by the W. A. Wilde Company, January 1954. https://www.west-point.org/users/usma1982/39622/NPC/LLS/lls.htm

[4] The N I V S t udy B i ble. N e w I n ternational V ersion, Z o ndervan B i ble Publishers, Copyright 1985 by The Zondervan Corporation (pg. 1725).

Made in the USA
Middletown, DE
13 November 2021